ALLERTON PARK INSTITUTE
Number 34

Papers Presented at the Allerton Park Institute

Sponsored by

University of Illinois
Graduate School of Library and Information Science

held

October 25-27, 1992
Allerton Conference Center
Robert Allerton Park
Monticello, Illinois

Evaluating Children's Books:
A Critical Look

*Aesthetic, social, and political aspects
of analyzing and using children's books*

BETSY HEARNE
and
ROGER SUTTON

Editors

University of Illinois
Graduate School of Library and Information Science
Urbana-Champaign, Illinois

© 1993 by the Board of Trustees of the University of Illinois
ISBN 0-87845-092-0

Printed in the United States of America on Acid-Free Paper

Acknowledgments

Leigh Estabrook, dean of the Graduate School of Library and Information Science, has been the prime mover in providing a new home for *The Bulletin of the Center for Children's Books* and in suggesting a conference at the Allerton Institute to celebrate our arrival at the University of Illinois, Urbana-Champaign. Professor Selma Richardson gave us valuable advice on conceptualizing and organizing the conference. Deborah Stevenson, assistant editor of *The Bulletin,* helped at every level along the way, including the design of the cover with Debra Bolgla's drawings. The GSLIS staff, especially Willa Reed, were indispensable, as were Jeff Sands, program director of conferences and institutes, and the staff of the Allerton Conference Center, who made us feel right at home in an elegant setting. Laurel Preece and Rhonda Gerber Arsenault have been endlessly cooperative in the transmutation of conference papers into monograph. Our thanks to you all.

CONTENTS

Introduction

In 1967, when I became a reviewer for *Booklist,* a grande dame named Edna Vanek had been the editor in chief since the year I was born. I thought she looked like the stereotypical librarian. Now I look exactly the same way, but then I was wearing bell-bottom jeans and wailing over the cartons after cartons of books that kept coming in. Finally, when five boxes of Franklin Watts books arrived on the same day, I went and flopped down in her office and said, "What am I going to do with all these books?" She looked at me with steely eyes and not a hair out of place and said, "Just take them one book at a time."

I still have the same problem today with all these books, and I don't know that I have a better solution. I've been a professional children's book reviewer for 25 years—which means that I've edited 20 volumes of book review journals and have dealt with about 100,000 new juvenile trade books outside of those I encountered in my earlier work as a school and public librarian. For 15 of those years, I have been in the acutely uncomfortable position of being reviewed as well as reviewing—which has occasioned some hypersensitivity about both camps. I've also spent 24 years being the parent of one or another young child, a phenomenon accounted for by having children far too far apart. And now I teach children's literature to college children who think that they are grown up, or I expound upon the importance of children's literature to university administrators and faculty members who think that *they* are grown up. And through it all, I continue to review about seven children's books a week. One a day. Just like I take my vitamins. Outside of the occasional nervous rash, the surest thing I have gleaned from all this is an awareness of seasonal, social, economic, and aesthetic cycles in children's books.

Juvenile publishing is in an unprecedented success cycle, which causes, ironically, unprecedented problems for creators, reviewers, and consumers of children's books. A popularized market has dictated more quantity and less quality control than ever before. Financial bonanzas have generated more glitz and less durability. Librarians, teachers, and reviewers come close to being overwhelmed by the sheer numbers and by the subsequent pressure to make choices quickly but effectively. Yet the process of evaluating a book takes just as long as it used to. The process of reading a book to a child takes just as long as it used to. And balancing a book budget takes a lot longer.

Selection now implies more selectivity than in any other time in the history of children's literature. In children's literature, selection depends primarily on reviews. Few professionals have access to examination centers that receive all the juvenile books published every year. Reviewing at every level, from the published journal to the list annotated by a librarian or school library staff, is more basic to this field than it is to any other. We are too new to have established a traditional canon, a Pulitzer Prize, a reliable best-seller list, or even a steady foothold of attention in the media. Yet children's literature has always been central to children's librarianship, and it has become, commendably, more central for teaching children in public and private schools. Evaluation is central to children's literature, and evaluation is most often evinced in reviews.

To review means, literally, to look again, from the French *revoir*. It is a reviewer's work to read a book, to look for deeper understanding, and to find a clear expression of that understanding. I would argue that all persons involved in evaluation and selection are, to some extent, reviewers. All reviewers must resist the pressure to slide over the surface, must push beyond the practical to reach critical perception.

Let me outline some of the problems I see in reviewing books, evaluating books, and consuming books. How do seasonal rushes and publishing cycles affect our reactions and even our judgment? How do we juggle points of view when the critic, reviewer, librarian, parent, and child voices within ourselves don't always agree? What do we do when quality, popularity, and usefulness conflict in the evaluation of a book? How do we weigh a summary recommendation when text and illustration vary in quality? How do we deal with interesting failures versus mediocre successes in reviewing children's books? How do we detect new trends, cycles, subjects, and styles? How do we deal with glamorous packaging and celebrity names? How do we stay in touch with kids? How do we balance immediate effects with long-term durability when speed and quantity pressure our reviews? How do we deal with social and political bias in a book? How do we deal with our own subjectivity? How do we deal with what we decide are controversial elements without censoring the book at the reviewing stage? What do we do as review editors when someone submits a review that we have real trouble with in terms of basic judgment? How do we avoid ruts and jading as reviewers? How do we deal with a broad scope of needs among our subscribers? How do we deal with subject specialties such as physics and hard sciences? And finally, lately, how do we balance aesthetic criteria with social pressures to be politically correct? We'd like to address some of these questions in the course of our conference on evaluating children's books. There are many answers to some, and there are no answers to others. To most questions, each reviewer—that is, each of us—must find her own answers—the more carefully considered the better. Welcome aboard.

Betsy Hearne
Editor

Censorship, Negative Criticism, Glitzy Trends, Growing Publisher Output, and Other Shadows on the Landscape of Children's Book Reviewing:

A Panel of Discussion Moderated by Roger Sutton (RS), with Ilene Cooper (IC), Betsy Hearne (BH), Trevelyn Jones (TJ), Joanna Rudge Long (JRL), and Anita Silvey (AS)

RS: I'd like to introduce you to the five members of our panel. Trevelyn Jones has been the *School Library Journal* book review editor since November of 1982 and prior to that worked for 16 years as a children's librarian on Long Island. Joanna Rudge Long has been the children's and YA editor of *Kirkus Reviews* since 1986. She was also a children's librarian at the New York Public Library and elsewhere before going to *Kirkus*. Anita Silvey has been the editor in chief of *The Horn Book Magazine* and *The Horn Book Guide* since 1984, and prior to that worked in children's book publishing and as an assistant editor at *The Horn Book*. Ilene Cooper has been the children's book editor of the American Library Association's *Booklist* since 1990 and has been a book reviewer there since 1981. Before that she was a librarian at the Winnetka Public Library in Illinois. Betsy Hearne has been editor of *The Bulletin of the Center for Children's Books* since 1985, before which she was children's book editor at *Booklist,* with experience as a school and public librarian.

I'd like to start by giving the editors a chance to discuss a little bit of their philosophy of reviewing. Trev?

TJ: School Library Journal is a very practical journal, and our philosophy is practical idealism. We're sifting, sorting, searching, and highlighting the best for each intended audience in terms of quality, appeal, and clarity of presentation. But we're not trying to be elitist. We're not trying to say, "Only the best." We're looking for things that kids will believe, kids will find popular, that will move, and that will also give a nice breadth and depth to a collection. We want to inform readers of a book's strengths and weaknesses with enough information so that our readers can make up their own minds. A book is strong here, it's weak here—you decide. We're giving you the best information we can. We can't make up your minds for you. Basically, what we're trying to do is build solid, strong working collections.

RS: Joanna?

JRL: My ultimate goal at *Kirkus* is, of course, to get the books to the children, and I think I try to do everything Trev tries to do. *Kirkus* goes mostly to public libraries, and I'm always aware of that, though I'd like to talk more to school libraries. First of all, I tell subscribers what I think they need to know—and what *they* think they need to know, with a few exceptions. For example, I don't dwell on sex and violence in the book unless there's something extraordinary about the fact that it's there. I care a lot about what gets to the kids, so I proselytize a little bit. Just as a good book can illuminate beyond its immediate subject, a review can also offer insights beyond the subject of the review. While I'm identifying high quality or usefulness or whatever, I also deliberately choose books that one way or another are problematic. Flawed books by fine writers are interesting, as are books that exemplify one sort or another of wrongheadedness, such as not respecting the audience or not respecting the material. A book may vandalize *The Elephant's Child,* which is regularly done; or a book about sugaring might put the wrong bark on a maple tree (I come from Vermont); or a book could have a generic sort of portrayal. A wonderful British picture book author, Martin Waddell, wrote a pseudo-American Laura Ingalls Wilder book that was really bland, but it also made me wonder how Americans view other cultures, how we've probably been equally guilty and don't see it as well when we're the culprits. Basically, I want to convey useful information and also make my readers think.

RS: Anita?

AS: A friend of mine, upon hearing that we were all going to be here at this panel, said, "A book critic is someone who goes around battlefields shooting the wounded." That gave me pause to reflect. What is it, after all, that we're engaged in when we're trying to evaluate books? Reviewing books for children is one of the most complex and subtle balancing acts that I know. I can talk about the process easily enough. You read and reread a book, usually privately and by yourself. And then most of us, either in conversation or more formal settings, get together and talk about that book and try to determine what we're going to do with it. What we consider when we review may be any one of a number of factors, and how important each factor is depends on the book.

I often think when I'm writing a review that there's a committee that sits in my head nattering away at me all the time. There's one member, the literary stylist, who may talk about the beauty of the writing, the quality of the artwork, how the book works as a piece of art. Next the pragmatist gets in and says, "Yes, but what about an index? What school curriculum will this fit into?" The pragmatist is shortly followed by the populist who says, "Will children read this? What children will read this? How popular will this book be?" There is the social scientist, or philosopher, who is arguing, "What does this book say to children? What values does it impart? What vision of life does it give?" And then, of course, there's always the voice of the child.

I have to make a confession. I'm like many other people in this profession. I put on a hat and walk out and try to act like an adult. If I play dress up, maybe you'll believe me. But within is that child who is always there, and that child's voice is always balanced by the adult critic who says, "I didn't like the last book by Gary Paulsen and I don't like this one." As an adult, what I have to do, after the nattering goes on, is to come to some decision about how all those factors are going to weigh in the review.

We have to give people enough information so that they can answer the question, "Do I want to take this book into my home, my school, my library, or bookstore?" All of the editors here have to produce journals and reviews under tremendous deadline pressure. We have to be able to walk, talk, chew gum, make phone calls, and write reviews at the same time. And then there you are, forever in print, with your best opinion of that book at that particular moment. The committee goes on meeting in my head. Children's responses to the book will change mine. Other adults' responses to the book will change mine. But the printed opinion remains the same.

I'd like to think that if there's justice in heaven, Anne Carroll Moore and E. B. White are in the same book discussion group. Anne is now a passionate advocate of his masterpiece, *Charlotte's Web,* and they're the best of friends. But every time you go back to her review in *Horn Book,* here on earth, alas, ACM still disapproves.

I'd like to believe that with a great deal of humility, with a tremendous caring for the people who work with children and for children themselves, and with a passion for books, we do our work to the best of our ability. I don't really think that book critics go around searching the battlefield. I think rather that what we try to do, in the words of Helen Gardner, is to "light the lamp to illuminate the darkness," first of all for ourselves, then for others.

RS: Ilene?

IC: With 6,000 children's books being published a year, it's sometimes very difficult to think of each book as an individual title. Usually in the spring and fall, you think of it as this gelatinous mass that's coming toward you, and it has to be cut into very tiny pieces. But my philosophy is to make each book an individual book. At *Booklist,* one thing that I have primary responsibility for is assigning books to reviewers, and I think both publishers and authors would be surprised at how much time I spend trying to get the right book to the right person, because it's a no-win situation if you just give a book to somebody at random. If you give Anita that Gary Paulsen book, it's not going to work. I also try to assess the book the way it was written. I try not to assess what I would like to have seen written or the better book that it could have been. Each book is an individual, and that's how you have to see it.

I may be kind of prejudiced in this direction because I'm a writer myself, so I've been on both sides of the reviewing process and I know that it's a lot easier to write reviews than it is to get reviewed. And I often say what any other writer says, "Reviewers—what a bunch of idiots." Which then chokes in my throat.

RS: Betsy?

BH: What I would campaign for most in reviewing is critical imagination. I think that we fault books for a lack of imagination and originality, but too often we fault those books in words that are clichés themselves. The most important thing is to stretch critically with every book. Sometimes you don't have to stretch very far, and the book itself dictates a pretty low-level review. Even there, if you back off and get some perspective on what the problem is and try to reach with your critical imagination, you can find new ways to think and write about a book. While we're struggling with all this very seriously, we have to keep a humorous perspective—and we have to keep deadlines. We are always caught between the pragmatic and the ideal.

RS: I began in the book reviewing field as Zena Sutherland's editorial assistant at *The Bulletin* when I was in library school. This was 10 years ago, and we were dealing with, maybe, 2,500 books a year. Now, as Ilene says, we're dealing with 6,000. I'd like to know how each of you copes with that incredible amount of material: what you select and how you select it. Also, if you could, tell me approximately how many books your journal reviews in a year.

TJ: We try and do as many as possible. Therefore, our reviews are very brief and to the point, and we try to keep plot and character description down. From January through October of 1992, we've reviewed 3,550. Figure 600 more for November and December, and you can see that we're reviewing around 4,100 a year now. Next year, we are increasing our page budget a little, so we will be doing more.

We review all individual titles from major publishers. There's no question about that. With a series coming in at 10, 20, or 30 volumes, I would do a selective sampling. I no longer promise to do every title in every series. With all of the new publishers coming up—and there are many of them—I try to do all of their first and second list and then I may have to ease off a little with their series titles.

JRL: *Kirkus* is doing about 1,500 a year; I don't have time to count. It's overwhelming because I'm sorting these by myself and sending them out by myself and I'm doing half the reviews or more; I don't count that either. I try to do everything people are really going to want to know about most. I can't possibly deal with all the series because I'm only one person, and they do begin to look an awful lot alike.

I think the individual books from the individual publishers are the hardest of all for me to let go, but sometimes I have to. I don't think I've given up on a *Henry and Mudge* book yet, but I did give up on *Amanda and Oliver Pig*. Is that right? The latest is a perfectly good book, but it's not that different from the others in the series. I try to sample all kinds of books—to do some negative reviews as well as positive ones. Obviously, I do mostly positive reviews because you don't want to know about bad books; you want to know about good books. But I do a few negative ones, partly because we don't always know until we review them how good or bad they are.

AS: When *The Horn Book Guide,* which is much more comprehensive than *Horn Book,* came into our lives, things got a little easier in terms of deciding what books to review, because we now have a series of checks and balances. The managing editor and I do an initial screening of all books. We then send those titles that we really find worthy out to our reviewers who are working with children. There is a staff of 10 book reviewers, and they are working with children in a variety of settings. Then we pass the book cart on to the editor of the *Guide.* Inevitably, she later comes into my office and says, "Well, you may have missed the Caldecott winner." She points out a few books that I've overlooked and that she really believes a *Horn Book* reviewer should see.

The remainder of the books we then send out to our *Guide* reviewers. We have close to 60 or 70 *Guide* reviewers, and most of them are busy reading all the time. They will do a reading and a review, and sometimes will say to us, "You know, this is good enough for *The Horn Book Magazine*. Maybe you should consider it." Then we send it to a *Horn Book* reviewer.

I have no limit on the number of books I can review at *Horn Book*. I'd love to have a publishing season where I reviewed every book published, but realistically it is somewhere within the range of 15 to 20% of whatever is published. If the numbers go up, the percentage tends to remain the same, so the percentage of what we find really good seems to remain the same no matter how many more books come out.

IC: Booklist, as many of you know, has a recommended-only policy, although we push the limits of that quite a bit: We do have a lot of negative criticism in the reviews, and we do occasionally review a book and say that we are not recommending it. Usually that's because either the subject matter or the author is so important we think you would like to know about it. We review between 3,000 and 3,500 books, and we deal with our series books in a unique way, I think.

All the series books are looked at, but then they are put in a series roundup, which has saved us, and we hope you, an enormous amount of work. We may be doing the same thing with series fiction—listing titles that we will not review, as a service, so that you will know if the next *Sweet Valley High* or *Baby-Sitters Club* has come out.

No journal is ever going to have the number of pages in a telephone book, and so, though we get more books to review, we are still going to be able to review only a certain percentage of them because we all have page budgets.

I think one of the nice things about *Booklist* is that we have an in-house staff that reviews approximately 50% of the books. We have about 20 outside reviewers to whom we can also send books, but it's particularly helpful, with books that we want to discuss or argue about, to have an in-house staff so we can all read a book and each get our say.

BH: The Bulletin reviews about 1,000 books a year, which used to be close to half and is now closer to a fifth or a sixth of what is published. It's something that I've been wrestling with lately, like Jacob wrestled with the angels. Fundamentally, my instinct is to be more selective and to keep the reviews critically imaginative. I think that we can no longer maintain the ideal of doing everything that we used to do. As children's literature becomes more like adult literature, we have to seek instead more venues for reviews. The problem here is that for practical use and critical consideration you have the same reliance on a very limited number of review journals, and yet you have this literature that's burgeoning in both numbers and in a kind of star-studded author/illustrator/best-seller syndrome. We're really at a crossroads and can no longer assume what we used to. We're going to have to make different choices and suffer the consequences. The more the publishers put out, the less we're going to be able to review because our pages basically have to stay the same, without expanded budgets and staff.

In terms of practical detail, Roger Sutton, Deborah Stevenson, and I do almost all the reviews, with occasional contributions by a school or public librarian. We select books for varied reasons. One reason is new trends. You all remember when books about child abuse appeared where there had never been books on that subject, or suddenly there were books about AIDS. I think we all try to pick up the books that might spearhead those trends.

We also review books that are important to curricula in schools, that are by important authors and illustrators, or that are first novels, because we want to encourage the development of new writers. We have begun to pass over those titles that appear to be gorgeous coffee-table books with little substance and text. If Barry Moser brings out 15 books a year, he is going to have to realize that there will be an effect. They may all be gorgeous, but we're going to have to be more and more selective about which gorgeous books of his we choose to review.

We choose books that we think will be controversial, and we also have an obligation to speak to those books that we think will be highly popular with children even if they stink critically. Any time there's a serious disagreement on the staff, we feel that that would probably represent a disagreement in the population, so we try to review that book.

We review negatively when we think that a book presents a problem important enough to take up space. Just to pick up another mediocre book and spend a lot of time saying what's wrong with it is not worth the space, but picking up a book that represents an issue and examining it is important.

RS: How do you handle disagreement? Whether it's a review from an outside reviewer that comes back and you think, "Did I read the same book?" or if it's someone in your office who, in fact, you respect a lot, but this time you just can't seem to come to an agreement? Who gets the last word?

TJ: School Library Journal's reviewers, as you probably know, are all volunteers. There are about 350 of them from schools and public libraries. I really respect their opinions, because they're the ones who are out there with the kids. We can sit around the office and say, "Is anybody going to read this?" and can call the reviewer and get an answer. We have three reviewers on almost every book: The reviewer reads it, our associate editor Luanne Toth reads it, and our freelancer who comes in once or twice a week also reads. There is no book, fiction or picture book, that has not been read by one of our staff members and the reviewer. (That's not true of all the nonfiction because we have specialists, and I wouldn't begin to tackle it all.) If one staff member disagrees with the review, the other one reads it. If the other one agrees with the reviewer, we let it go. If we both disagree with the reviewer, we call and basically ask the reviewer to explain a little bit more about his or her position. We're not really trying to talk them into coming around our way but trying to get more into their thinking, what they're seeing that we're not. If they give a very solid reasoning for their review, if they give us a point that we have not really thought of, we will go with that review. If we find that there's a hidden agenda there or that the reasoning is really not grounded in fact, or the reviewer is saying, "I really don't like this book and I don't know why," or "I'm really not willing to come out with a negative review. I don't want to hurt anybody's feelings," then we will say, "Look, I'm sorry, but this is not really a book for you," and it will be taken over in the office. That might happen once or twice a year. Almost always we come to an agreement.

JRL: Even though there are a number of people who contribute reviews to *Kirkus*, I revise the reviews a great deal more and standardize the prose probably more than anyone else here does. It's not that I don't rely on the reviewers for their judgment. I'm most likely to entirely overrule somebody who's new, who maybe will grow to work better, or maybe we'll give up on each other after a few tries. When I get to know a reviewer very well, sometimes if I find I'm in disagreement and I trust the reviewer's judgment, I'll say, "Well, heck, you know, it's time for this reviewer to have his or her say," and I'll go with their judgment even when I disagree with it—not if it's a major philosophical difference, but if it's of a lesser degree. But basically I have the final say, and I do make a lot of changes.

AS: Our review staff gets together and we hash all of this out in a review meeting where we decide what's going to go into each issue of the magazine. The reviewers present the books they're going to review and have to convince the other reviewers and me that they should review them. These meetings are very lively, as you might imagine, and we really argue books out. If we can't reach a consensus at that point, we pass the books around to everybody, go back and read them, and come back again and argue about it. However, even with all of that, in the end there's going to be disagreement over books.

My general philosophy is that if a reviewer can really present a strong opinion as to why that book should be reviewed, and they are personally enthusiastic, I know there are going to be other readers out there who are, too. I believe book taste is individual taste. In the same way, if somebody's unduly prejudiced against a book, I will quickly move it to another reviewer. The minute they say, "I just hate cat books," I say, "Thank you for sharing that with me," and give it to someone else.

I had to pull *The Relatives Came* from a lovely reviewer. She thought there was too much kissing and hugging, and I knew it was just the wrong match. Things like that happen, but we really try to take care of it up front and fight it out with each other. The books that end up making a great impact are usually the ones we fight about the most. We fought like cats and dogs over *Where the Wild Things Are*—very often controversy about a book is a good sign.

Our reviewer of *The Stinky Cheese Man* says it's a masterpiece, and when she brought it to a review meeting, she was surprised to find that some of her colleagues thought it should be rejected outright and never see the light of day. We fought about it. There were some people who thought it was too adult, too sophisticated; it's making jokes that kids aren't going to understand. When we have that kind of disagreement, we take it back to the classroom, back to the library; we test our theories.

I don't know about you, but if I love a book, I can sell it; and if I hate it, I can make it not go. When we are this passionate about books, negative or positive, even testing the book may not be the best case. The reviewer who hated it is in a working-class public library, and she said it's great for private school students but it'll never work with her kids. She thought it was a class thing altogether. She had no success with it in the library. A private school librarian, who loved it, said that all she would have to do is get up and sell it. And somebody who was in between had a little success. Now again, these are different audiences, different kids, different responses. So that didn't solve our dilemma with the book at all.

In the end, as I said, we star by consensus. I have to have a strong consensus. The majority of the reviewers really loved this book. They think it's terrific. My guess is that if I've got six out of ten reviewers who like it, probably six out of ten subscribers are going to like it, and the other four of you are not going to be enthusiastic about it at all and will wonder why in the world all of these journals are starring this particular book. I think every review journal has starred *The Stinky Cheese Man*, but my guess is it's going to be one of the titles about which somebody is going to say, "What do these reviewers smoke at lunch?"

IC: At *Booklist*, there's occasionally blood in the halls, but not too often. We each have our own books to review. The in-house reviewers generally make their own decisions, although there's certainly a lot of discussion. If people ask our opinions, they get them. The outside reviewers all live in the Chicago area, so it's pretty easy to call them up. But Stephanie Zvirin, Sally Estes (the manager of the department), and I do the editing. If a book comes in and we're looking at the book and it doesn't seem to match the review, we take it to one another and say, "What do you think?" If there's a disagreement, we then call the reviewer, and, as the others have said, see if he or she can make a strong case. Reviewing is an individual decision. I very rarely override somebody unless I have a strong opinion or else I'm not getting a response from them that satisfies me. Usually, it's amicably worked out in a phone conversation, to my satisfaction anyway.

BH: The first thing I say is, "Prove it. Give me the evidence for your opinion here," which is an old academic trick that makes people articulate more clearly what they mean. And if they can do that, then even if I disagree, I would let that opinion stand.

I try to give the book the benefit of the doubt in the sense of giving it to the reviewer who I think would treat it with the greatest respect. But when I hear all of what we're doing—this cross-checking and consensus and coddling that's going on here and compare that to the way adult books are treated—I'm amazed.

What I'd like to speak to is the lack of negative reviewing in this field. Publishers are shocked when they read negative reviews of children's books, partly because they're not used to it. I know that the publishers in the audience will probably disagree with that, but compared to adult books, which get slammed up, down, and sideways by somebody from way out in left field who has no expertise in the subject whatsoever, we are dealing very carefully and idealistically with these books, giving them a lot of time and a lot of space.

At *The Bulletin*, the three of us fight about books all the time. I, for the first time in a long time, had to abstain this week from taking a vote on a book, *The Huron Carol*, by de Brébeuf. It's a perfectly decent book in terms of both art and historical text. Here's a hymn about the baby Jesus put into Native American terms by a French priest in the 17th century—and I just go haywire. That's my first signal: watch it. I'm saying, "How *dare* he. How dare this priest come in and lay his religion on these people and some publisher says, 'Oh, this is great. We'll put it in a children's book,' instead of actually taking the Huron mythology itself and putting that in." Well, I knew immediately, as soon as I heard myself say this, that I had gone around the bend. It doesn't mean that I gave up my opinion, but it does mean that I let Roger review the book and say . . .

RS: I loved it.

BH: He's Catholic!

Anyway, I'd like to raise an issue beyond this specific book, which is the conflict between aesthetic criteria and political correctness.

RS: Well, I have a question from the audience, which I think none of you would like to deal with, but let's: "Richard Peck said at an ALA conference that we judge a book by the race of the author, and that's horrifying. I heard someone comment that we've been doing that for years, it just isn't working in his favor right now."

TJ: I heard that speech, and I must say I agree with Richard's point, that an author has a right to create a character the way he wants to, as he wants to, whatever race, whatever nationality, whatever sex. I think that we're getting a little bit too involved in political correctness in terms of the author's rights, and I'm seeing it particularly in novels. It seems that these days, you simply cannot have a villain who is black, you cannot have a villain who is Native American, you can't have a villain who is a boy, you can't have a villain who is a girl. Nowhere can you have a villain but in science fiction and fantasy, if they're aliens! I think we're taking too many rights away. I certainly think we should maintain our standards of sensitivity, but let's remember that people have a right to create what they want to.

JRL: If someone who is white cannot create a black character, or someone who is black can't create a white character, we can't have multiracial casts in any single book. Books will become segregated. I think we treat all children's books rather tenderly, and I think we treat books that come from minority groups or historically under-privileged groups with particular tenderness when it comes to reviewing them, partly because we are so desperate to have books in these areas and we want to nurture the authors and the illustrators, but partly because it's become a habit, and we need to take care about that and begin to impose the same sorts of standards there that we do elsewhere.

RS: I was asking an editor I know about publishing books on minority subjects and she said, "Yeah, we will publish a book on a minority subject, even when we know it isn't up to our usual standard." Do you feel that the review journals coddle a book because of its subject or the need for the book?

AS: Whether it's books on minorities or books on semiconductors, I think there's always that tendency for us to say, "Well, it's the only thing we have, and therefore . . . what do we do with it?" We tend to give something like that a little extra credence. But we need to get involved in the artistic questions of this. Are the characters believable? Who cares who created them—do they have authenticity? It's those sorts of things which we really try to address rather than looking at the back flap to see whether there's a picture of the author.

IC: I can tell you two recent anecdotes. I was reviewing a book called *Where the Broken Heart Still Beats,* which is the story of Cynthia Ann Parker, who was a white woman abducted by the Comanches and then returned against her will. Her family found her and made her go back with them to Texas. The author, Carolyn Meyer, gives a very harsh picture of the Comanches. They're scalping, they're keeping slaves, they're being Comanches, I guess, according to the way she was describing them. Now, of course, she did have Cynthia Ann Parker longing to return to her people, to her Indian people, so there was a balance there, but I found myself getting very nervous about this. And I didn't like that feeling . . . "Well, is this right? Is this politically correct?" Another book came in, a picture book about an African-American family, and they're on a picnic. They were eating catfish, and in the pictures, they were shown to be barefoot. One of our white publishing assistants came to us and said, "This is a terrible book. You can't review this book. It's politically incorrect. I think this review is absolutely wrong." Well, the review had been done by an African-American reviewer who thought it was a charming book.

BH: I don't like that word, *charming.*

IC: It was a *lovely* book.

BH: One of our typical arguments. But seriously, the Carolyn Meyer book was full of villains; most of the white people were unsympathetic characters, too. I was at a conference and I heard a whole series of Native American speakers get up and say, "Stop idolizing us as these wondrous nature-loving, ecologically perfect, 19th-century beings." It reminded me that the greatest cultural portrayals, the best-crafted and most deeply realized characterizations, always involve good and bad. When you see a portrayal of a perfect person—and there are way too many too-good people in children's literature—you know that this writer has not gone to the next level, hasn't peeled off the skin of the onion. That has to be criticized, no matter what color the reviewer or what color the writer.

TJ: I would just like to add one point to that. We realize that a lot of our subscribers are desperate for minority books. That doesn't mean that we're going to give those books a positive review. It doesn't mean we're going to say that they're good books. What we will say is that this is a book about a black or Native American family, but if it's a mediocre book, the decision is in your ballpark. We're not trying to make up your minds for you. We've given you the information we think you need to make up your own minds.

BH: I think that a lot of current publishing takes advantage of nervousness about political correctness. I cannot tell you the number of revisionist Columbus books I reviewed over the last year. Some of them are very solid research, but some of them are so calculating in playing on p.c. sensitivities that after a while, you just sit back and say, "I'm going to have to be pretty calculating about this review." Ultimately, I base my judgment on aesthetic criteria. One book that I liked quite a bit but still had some trouble with was *Morning Girl* by Michael Dorris, which was a fantastic portrayal of a Taino family, but which I thought introduced unnecessarily, at the very end, an excerpt from Columbus's journal, which says something to the effect that maybe these people can even learn to speak someday—ironic after the family's complex, rich development. It seemed like a gimmick, and I didn't think he needed it. There are a lot of reviewers who disagree with me about that.

I also had trouble with Patricia Polacco's *Chicken Sunday,* which is a real pitch for intercultural understanding, but I thought it worked way too hard at intercultural understanding and not hard enough at portraying individuals.

IC: I disagree with some of those, but I'll go on to my own pet peeves. I review a lot of the religion books at *Booklist,* and I think in general both publishing and reviewing do a pretty poor job on religion books because nobody wants to get into too much controversy and nobody wants to take a stand, so you get lots of versions of Noah's Ark and not much else.

We receive letters asking, "Why don't you review more Christian books?" We are making an effort. Obviously, our subscribers want to have those books reviewed. And, of course, some are well written, some are not, and each has to be judged on its individual merits.

Anyway, the book that I had problems with is called *David's Songs: His Psalms and Their Stories.* Colin Eisler has taken about 46 of the psalms and rewritten them. Some people have a problem with dumbing down the psalms, and I am one of them. A psalm about being jealous—David's looking at people who have more that he does—has the last three lines rewritten as, "Whatever they say is mean and nasty. How could they get so rich when they are so bad?" There's a clonker for you. It's just not quite the way David might have written it. Yet it's actually a beautiful book. The pictures are quite lovely, and it's a prime piece of bookmaking. So here was a publishing effort that really went the extra mile, tried to produce something that was original, did a very nice piece of bookmaking, as I said, but . . . was the concept wrong to begin with? When we get a book like this, we really have to judge it on all of those elements and discuss them in the review. We try to give all the information, and then it's up to the librarian to be the final arbitrator. The kids are the ultimate readers, but the librarian makes the decision about buying the book. Hopefully, we don't confuse you more than enlighten you.

TJ: What do you do when two of your favorite books of the year seem to be without an audience? Either because of format, design, subject matter, or mixed purpose? The writing is magnificent—witty, clever, everything you could ever want. Unfortunately, it doesn't seem to fit the audience. This is the problem I found—first of all, with William Brooke's *Untold Tales,* which I wish I could say was the next step up after *Stinky Cheese.* It's the story of a prince, and Beauty and the Beast, and the Sleeping Beauty. You will all love it. I will say even seventh or eighth graders might love it (although I'm not sure how much they are into middle-age marriages gone stale). Unfortunately, the format is not going to attract anyone in seventh or eighth grade. My reviewer did try it with kids, and she could not get it off the shelf. She could booktalk it, and she could read it aloud, but she couldn't get anybody to want to take it out and read more. They were happy with what she read to them, but it was, "No, no, thanks."

Another book that falls into very much the same category is Bruce Brooks' *What Hearts.* This is obviously written from the heart. It must have been a very painful book to write, and I think that fact has made some holes in it that are going to leave great gaps for kids. It's also, I think, the type of book that you read, and you look back, and you understand what he was going through. But without the experience, I don't think you would. I'd love anybody else's thoughts on this one because I like the book so much. I'd like to be talked into the fact that it could be a children's book.

RS: As you may know, at *The Bulletin* we have a code system. And we have the code SpR—that's sort of our "way out" clause. It basically means, "We like this book a lot, but we wonder who else will."

My own agenda for the big problem these days is picture books for adults. They're labelled as picture books for all ages, but I think that "all ages" probably starts at about 35. *Orpheus,* by Charles Mikolaycak, is a very sexy, glamorous, sterile—I think—retelling of a Greek myth. Or there's the *Messiah,* with fancy pictures by Barry Moser. Keep in mind that of all the journals here, at least one of them has liked one of these books, so there's no agreement on what books actually fall into this kind of glitzy category. We all have our favorites.

Moser's illustrations accompany the text that Handel and his librettist used from Bible verses, and they really don't mean anything without the music, and they certainly don't mean anything to young children. "Rejoice greatly, O Daughter of Zion, shout, O Daughter of Jerusalem; behold, thy King cometh unto thee: He is the righteous Saviour; and He shall speak Peace unto the Heathen." It's beautiful, but what's it going to mean to a nine-year-old?

JRL: Then don't give it to a nine-year-old. I gave it to the conductor of my chorus, who's directing the *Messiah.* There are a lot of people who've sung the *Messiah,* and there are a lot of kids who won't listen to the *Messiah.* I think it's too bad to fault a book for the audience that it never sought—if it is a fine book, doing what it set out to do.

TJ: Our reviewer felt that this was definitely a book for grades nine and up. I think we have a problem when we start insisting that picture books be only for preschoolers or primary grades. As adults, we go to art museums, we appreciate art, but suddenly picture books are supposed to be for someone third grade and under. I think there are plenty of them for older readers. One of my friends uses picture books with her junior high class. I think that for books like this we need to *find* the audience.

AS: Is there no audience, or is there simply a small audience? And if there's a small audience, is it worth getting the book to those special readers who might appreciate the art? I think there is a core of books which need some attention drawn to them and which, put in the right hands, can make a difference with readers. We have to stay away from making book evaluation a popularity contest. If it were, we would all review the same things, and we all know what they would be. (I think it's terrific *The Bulletin* can do that special reader code, by the way.) But I would agree with Roger on these picture books. I've not a lot of patience with any of them. It's an unfortunate use of the picture book format.

IC: The trend I've seen that I find so discouraging is picture books with wonderful art and no story. I've talked to publishers about it; I know that some say, "Look, we want to keep these artists in our stable, and they don't want to share royalties with an author. . . ." It can be a financial thing. But to have beautiful artwork and no story with it is, I think, a waste of paper and a waste of all our time.

BH: I also see a very calculating use among children's book publishers of big adult names to do mediocre work, such as Amy Tan's *The Moon Lady* and James Michener's *South Pacific.* If a child had never heard

South Pacific, this book would not make him or her want to. The text is like lead falling, clunk, clunk, clunk to the floor on your foot. The illustrations are awkward; the people look like there's something wrong with their limbs.

That's another great problem I have today with picture books. Too many artists can't draw, especially the human figure; what we see over and over is amazingly awkward drafting. It's hidden in this particular book by a lot of wild color, just as the poor writing is hidden by a story for which many adults have great nostalgia. I think this is a perpetration of fraud on children.

The Amy Tan story was terrific in context. It originated in *The Joy Luck Club*—but it has been re-rendered into a picture book that's awkward and much too long, without the tonal shades of the original. It's all right to encourage responsible adult writers to try to write for children, but remember that this is done at the expense of developing unknown writers and illustrators with enormous talent to work with children's literature, *within* children's literature. The star-studded system is a real danger. The idea that you pay huge advances to people who you know are going to bring in a lot of money because of their name is something relatively new to children's literature, and it's scary.

IC: Although I agree that this is very calculated by the publishers, I think that libraries are probably not the audience they're looking for with these books. They're looking for the bookstore audience. Parents and grandparents who walk into a bookstore will go for Amy Tan. And then there's Whoopi Goldberg's picture book. The story is a horror, but the artwork for it is great. I said in my review, "Gee, at least we get this brand new artist who should go on doing books, and Whoopi Goldberg should go back to doing talk shows." But the bookstore is the primary audience for a lot of these, because librarians will read the reviews that ask, "Why is this book in existence?"

BH: Yet when people come into the library and ask for these books, it's a library's dilemma, after all. And a teacher's dilemma.

JRL: Whether it's the publisher who initiates it or the best-selling author who wants to write a children's book, there seems to be no conception of what a children's book is or what a child is. These books are often condescending and clichéd, as if, "I'm doing it for the little ones now, and I throw everything I know about writing out the window."

IC: In the publishers' defense, sometimes these adult authors say they want to do a children's book, and the publishing company doesn't want to offend them and says, "Okay, do a children's book."

AS: We could tell the publishers something very important if we all reviewed, bought, and gave a lot of attention to new authors and illustrators, but the reality is that we don't buy new authors. And we don't give new authors the review attention that we give the new Chris Van Allsburg.

RS: I think great picture books do fine whether they're by veterans or newcomers. But I don't think fiction by anybody—hardcover, children's, or YA fiction—is doing well at all. And here's a question from the audience on *nonfiction:* Does the need for subject outweigh flaws in style and other literary aspects?

BH: I think that reviewing any piece of nonfiction is a very delicate balance between how useful it's going to be and how good it is. As a librarian in a school where teachers said to their students, "You have to have three sources on this, that, and the other," at some points I would have bought almost anything—in spite of my critical training. I hate to say that about myself, but I think it would be the same story now. As a reviewer, I have to factor that experience in. On the other hand, the critical voice still plays, and the only thing you can do is say, book by book, "Here's what's good about this, here's what's bad about it, I wish it were better organized, but for those of you who need it, here it is."

TJ: The reason we do only a few titles in a nonfiction series, rather than list all of them, is that we find so many differences in quality, in accuracy, and in the ability to present information. Rather than just list them as a series and say, "Here they are," we'd rather do a few and show you the varying quality in them. We'll say, "This one's good, this one's bad, this one's mediocre," so that you can really see that they're not all of the same quality.

IC: When we look at our series roundup, we simply discard the books that don't meet our standards.

RS: Now, let me introduce a question from this audience about an earlier point. "Why do European-Americans always want to take the right to create books about people of color, no matter how stereotyped or reflective of long-standing cultural oppression? If people of color did not protest these, we would have lots of books of the ilk of *Ten Little Niggers*, etc. Look around. Look who selects what to review and how it is reviewed. Look at this audience. This is one reason the Coretta Scott King Award was established. The dialogue you hear is what happens all the time. Look who is deciding what is, quote, 'politically correct.'" Any comment?

AS: When we review, we really try, in all instances, to get a reading from someone of the group that's being represented. The review may not be written by a person from that group, but we will get input. We're all white women editors, of a particular age and background. If we want books for all of our children, we have to reach out for those with other sensibilities.

JRL: I have sent books for review to people of the relevant group, and I worry about it when I can't, which happens sometimes because of time constraints. I imagine that's why I tend to be overthoughtful— I worry about it a lot.

TJ: We try to get an ethnic book to librarians who are working in communities with that ethnic group. It may not necessarily mean that the librarian is of that ethnic group, but at least we are trying to reach the communities where he or she will know ethnic patrons and be able to test the book. Don't forget that our 350 reviewers or more are *out* there. We're reviewing fewer than four books a month in-house. Everything else is reviewed by librarians in the field.

IC: We also have librarians in the field, as Trev said, working with various cultures, and we do try and get a reading. We also have men— that other minority. You can never have the balance you want. But we certainly do our best to see that the book gets out to the people who want to know about it and who can give us a good reading on it.

BH: I think it's racist to feel that all the members of any particular group would agree on a book. I am reminded of *Jake and Honeybunch Go to Heaven,* which split the African-American urban community of Chicago every which way. Some hated it, some loved it, some resented it. I think it would be insulting to hand a book about the African-American experience to an African-American reviewer and say, "Do this because you're African-American, and this is about African-Americans." Every group has a great range of individual voices.

    The reason all of us up here are women is because, traditionally, men would not have the job. The reason that publishing for children is dominated by women is because men thought children were women's work. And now that publishing has become so financially profitable, a lot more males are being attracted into publishing, writing, and illustrating for children—so, there *is* a power operative here, a power of politics.

    But I am not happy with the idea that in order to write a book about lizards, you have to be a lizard, or in order to review a book about lizards, you have to be a lizard. There is a valid criticism to be leveled against reviewers or review editors who don't listen to a lot of different voices. You can only be what you are, no matter what color or what religion, and you have a right to an opinion, but your opinion acquires more validity the more open-minded you are and the more you listen to other people.

RS: "What can reviewing journals do to help librarians deal with self-censorship and precensorship pressures?"

IC: This has always been a really sticky question because you don't want to damn a book, but you want to give a fair representation of what it is. I think we're not doing our job if we don't tell our readers, "This is in the book," or "That is in the book," whether it's obscene language or incidents—in the briefest way possible sometimes. The thing we get the most unhappy letters about is not telling librarians about something in the book that is going to be a surprise to them when the parent comes and objects to it. If a mention of controversy is in a review praising a book, I don't think that's going to kill the book. But you make the decision. You know your patrons, you know your library; I just think it's our job to alert you to what you can expect, and what your patrons can expect.

JRL: Yes, but the line keeps changing, and we all have to keep renegotiating that line. I just got a complaining letter from somebody about a review published in 1975.

AS: Obviously in reviewing we're trying to be as honest as we can about what's there, but I am amazed at what people find in books to get upset about. *Daddy's Roommate* might become the great controversy on television, but we had no trouble reviewing it at all. We gave it a five in the *Guide* and just said, "If you have to have material on this topic, it's probably the only thing available."

RS: Is a five good or bad, Anita?

AS: It's bad. Six is the lowest.

RS: Why did you give it a five?

AS: It just wasn't a good story, but we had no problem with the subject. The things that will be upsetting in one community are not the things that are going to be upsetting in another community.

Chris Van Allsburg has taken on the whole witchcraft/devil issue with his book, *The Widow's Broom,* and we will no doubt have a lot of people objecting to it in certain places. But all we can really do is talk about that book as we see it.

I sometimes assume that most censorship cases come from people who are not very literate because they don't see something in context, or they don't see something in nuance, or they don't see subtleties. But even people who are literate and used to reading books can never read a book the same way. You try to be as honest as you can about the content of a book. But my guess is you yourself won't even know what book in the collection is going to cause controversy.

RS: But when we say, for example, something about page 19 where Deenie masturbates, etc., there are librarians out there who are going to say, "Whoa! I'm not getting near this book!" either because of personal distaste or knowledge that someone in their community will have trouble with it. I'm not quite sure how we can avoid that because we can't lie to make you buy a book and have you surprised at what might pop up inside.

TJ: Just one more thought on it: Read a lot of reviews if you've got a censorship case. Don't be afraid to buy a book if it's gotten good reviews, and if you get into problems, call us. We have backfiles and can support you with reviews. So, don't feel like you're out there all by yourself because a book you bought three years ago backfired. I just got a complaint about Greene's *I Know You, Al,* published in 1976.

IC: We got the same one. It's interesting, when I looked up our review of *I Know You, Al,* it said, this is a wonderful book, and funny, and there are scenes and language that are going to upset some people. Now I'm not sure what the librarian will do with that, but the review was honest.

RS: Trev said something that I would just like to expand on for a moment. You can't rely on one review source, and I think none of us would say, "Just read us." I remember Hazel Rochman telling me that she ran into a woman once who said, "Oh, when I see 'HR' at the end of a review, I know I can buy it." And Hazel said, "I pity that woman's library." So you really do need to keep widely abreast of the different journals.
   One more question: "How do you separate liking a book because you are personally interested in the subject and liking it because of its own qualities?"

BH: Actually, it's not that big a disadvantage to be personally involved in the subject. I get all the southern books, and I probably give them the benefit of the doubt because I'm interested in that region, and obviously from it, as you can hear from my accent when I get tired. What you have to watch more closely is what you hate. You can begin to feel what triggers overreactions. Then you back off and give the book to another person.

IC: I think one quality a reviewer should try to acquire is the willingness to be surprised. Sometimes we take books on subjects we're not particularly interested in to see if the book will grab us. It's almost a better test of a book than picking a subject that you like. And if it does grab you, then it certainly says something about the book.

AS: Reviewing is a balancing act. All of us have something we're irrationally passionate about. I love American history. I love to read it and review it and work with it. If you read a lot in an area, you can become a better reviewer. The great advantage to having passions is that you know an awful lot of books that have been done in that area, and you know how to rate them.

But I sometimes hear in my own voice a tone that warns, "Wait a minute, maybe this has more to do with me than it has to do with the book." If you're lucky, you know your own blind spots, and the longer you review, the better you learn them. Yet things come up and grab you by the ankles; a book you would never predict might upset you. I am amazed at what sets me off. What's so important in reviewing is having colleagues you can talk to, who will keep you in line, who will tell you that this little fluffy bunny book is just a fluffy bunny book. "I know you like bunnies, Anita, but . . ."

JRL: Reviewing is a great job. You have to know everything, and you have to go on trying to learn everything forever and ever. I learn some really neat things by doing books on subjects I know nothing about; at least I can tell if they're clear. But what's caught me up sometimes is doing something I thought I knew a lot about, like where I grew up, and finding I have to do a little fact-checking on myself to make sure I'm still right about these things I thought I knew. It turned out, for instance, that there was more than one kind of a mule's tail. When I complained, "That's not a mule's tail, that's a horse's tail," somebody found me a photo that proved the children's book was right, in spite of the fact that the drawing in the dictionary looked just like what I thought it should. Hunh!

JANICE N. HARRINGTON

Head of Youth Services
Champaign Public Library and Information Center
Champaign, Illinois

Children's Librarians, Reviews, and Collection Development

INTRODUCTION

In the 1990s, libraries are beginning to face the new demands of demographic and technological change. In this evolving context, a discussion of book reviewing and collection development can begin by examining the contemporary role of children's collections and of children's librarians in collection development.

As demography and technology change, children's librarians remain influential mediators between children and the books they read (England & Fasick, 1987, pp. 23-24). Although children's librarians' role as mediator has declined with their reduced purchasing power and the growth of direct marketing, libraries still purchase over half the children's books sold in the United States (England & Fasick, 1987, p. 24). To a considerable extent, then, librarians decide which books are available to children. In an information society, where it has become a truism that knowledge is power, access to print and nonprint media empowers children. Children's librarians should not underestimate, therefore, the importance of their knowledge of children's literature (Huntoon, 1992); nor should they underestimate their power to shape the information, literature, and communication media to which children will have access.

Literature gives children a means to explore human behavior safely and vicariously (Huck, Hepler, & Hickman, 1987, pp. 8-9). If a collection does not provide a broad range of literature, then it limits the ability of library users to participate in the depth and range of experience that, often, only reading will lead them to. A children's collection needs

27

materials that will help children answer the questions related to being human, that will help them compete academically, and nurture their reading interests, encourage them to pursue new interests, and hook them on the habit and pleasure of reading. At a time when so many schools are underfunded, and children in many rural and urban areas do not have equal access to high-quality education, the public library children's collection can become even more important. By making the best possible purchasing and selection decisions, librarians can provide more children with equal access to a major educational tool.

THE CHILDREN'S COLLECTION

The children's collection is at the center of the services that libraries offer, but it faces an increasing number of pressures. One of the greatest new pressures is the rapid increase in children's book publishing. There are simply more paperback series, picture books, nonfiction titles, and problem novels to choose from. Librarians, as well as booksellers, feel overwhelmed by the flood of new children's books. Projected sales for 1990 nearly doubled sales for 1985 (Simora, 1991, p. 23). While the market for children's books has increased, the purchasing power of children's librarians has declined. Publishers no longer rely on the library and school market to generate profits now that they have so much larger a market among the general public. Direct marketing has created new demands and the production of formats and sizes that are not designed for library collections.

As the market changes, so do the demands of readers. Public library use has increased across the board, including use by children. In 1988, 37% of users were 14 or younger (Eberhart, 1991, p. 193). Not only are more children using libraries, but also more of them ask for books from the newly growing segments of the expanding market, such as paperback mystery, horror, and romance series. With the new emphasis educators and librarians put on reading and literature in the home, and perhaps with the publication of tools like *The Read-Aloud Handbook* by Jim Trelease (1985), parents are more aware of the importance of literature and reading. They come to libraries wanting not only the familiar classics that they remember from their own childhoods but also the books that they find in their local bookstores or advertised in the media. Bookstores and book clubs are whetting the interest of children as well as parents. Children want the pulp paperbacks their friends are reading and the many series and spin-offs they discover in the bookstores. The electronic media continue to entice readers who see *Beauty and the Beast* or *Robin Hood* or *Reading Rainbow* and then expect the library to carry the same titles. Such changes especially affect public libraries because public libraries carry a higher percentage of fiction than school libraries.

Readers' demands are also changing because the readers themselves are changing. By 2010, one-third of Americans will be African-, Hispanic-, Native-, or Asian-American. Children and parents from these emerging majorities will bring distinct interests and needs to library collections.

Curriculum changes and new educational trends also affect purchasing needs. The focus on reading comprehension and the shift to literature-based education have changed the way teachers use libraries. In order to meet teachers' needs, children's librarians have to go beyond the age-old battle of trying to get teachers to tell them their assignments ahead of time and beyond the constant struggle to purchase enough multiple copies for classroom demand. They need to establish ongoing communications with school administrators, curriculum committees, and school media specialists. It is not enough to be prepared for isolated assignments. Librarians need the information that will help them match their collection to the curriculum. They need to know the scope and sequence of what is being taught and at what grade level, as well as what resources teachers already have in their schools. The movement towards a "literature-driven curriculum," which focuses on communicating "culture through literature," on providing "students a continuing experience with real books—the kind they will read outside school," and on individual reading choices, has put new demands on libraries to go even farther to collect multicultural materials and meet a wide range of individual reading interests (Smith, 1989, p. 720). The home-schooling movement is also producing growing demands on many collections, because home educators require special curriculum materials and are heavy library users.

THE ROLE OF THE CHILDREN'S LIBRARIAN

Other issues affecting collection development include funding and the changing demands on children's librarians. As funding goes up and down, many materials go unpurchased or unreplaced, so that collections come to represent the feasts and famines of varying budgets. Furthermore, over half of public libraries (58%) have no librarians whose primary job is to serve children, 34% have only one children's librarian, and only 8% have two or more children's librarians (Eberhart, 1991, p. 194). The expectations for children's librarians have increased and changed even from what they were 10 years ago. Those librarians who are fortunate enough to have staffs must be middle managers, deal with a myriad of personnel issues, and participate in the management of the library as a whole. As demographics change, services move outside the library. Librarians are asked to get involved in their communities, to network, and to build coalitions with other childcare agencies. As Cummins (1989) writes,

> the children's librarian and school media specialist are the Renaissance people of the profession. You are expected to know how to run the children's department, know the children's materials both print and nonprint, plan programs, work at the adult reference desk to help cover the schedule (or fill in in the classroom), know the best-sellers and adult reference materials, understand computers and automation, provide outreach to the community, know how to deal with teenagers, have competent managerial skills, often serve as second in command, and smile as you try to cram sixty hours of work into a thirty-five to forty hour work week. (pp. 38-39)

These growing demands mean that time—especially for the 34% who have to work alone—has often become as scarce as the dollars that make up their declining budgets.

Together these concerns affect librarians' work in four areas. First, librarians are increasingly concerned with accountability. They must be able to justify spending choices to their administrations, and that requires a systematic approach to collection development.

Second, in this complex environment, a children's librarian can no longer effectively determine a budget, build a collection, or make efficient and practical use of reviews without a written collection development policy. As Gorman and Howes (1989) write: "A library collection is not merely an assembly of books, not even an assembly of good books; they have to relate to each other" (p. 18). Collection development policies help define the purpose of collections. They help set spending priorities and, just as important, they help librarians follow through on the priorities they set. Moreover, as staffs change, a written policy helps protect collections from the shifting whims of individual librarians' tastes and biases.

Third, librarians need to know what their users want and who their users are. Children's librarians use a variety of techniques to assess patron interest, including reference logs, in-house surveys, suggestion boxes, files of teachers' assignments, and personal contact with patrons. *Output Measures for Public Library Service to Children* is one landmark tool now available to help gather information about library users (Walters, 1992).

Fourth, as librarians find themselves becoming more selective in order to meet the evolving needs of their collections and patrons, reviews can be a crucial tool for making their selections serve the requirements of an ongoing collection policy.

REVIEWS AND CHILDREN'S LIBRARIANS

How successfully any review journal meets the needs of children's librarians often depends upon how well its reviewers understand that there are highly particular things that children's librarians want from reviews and, therefore, that there are also particular things they want from reviewing journals. Librarians want reviews to appear promptly, to be brief, and to select materials assertively. They need promptness because patrons ask for books as soon as those books appear in local bookstores and reading clubs. They need brevity because professional librarians place immense value on their time. Busy librarians must often bring review journals home, where they can find blocks of undisrupted time. Therefore, reviews must be concise and bottomline oriented. Reviews that merely focus on plot summaries, that use vague language, or that turn into showcases for the reviewers' wit hamper a professional's ability to do his or her job. Reviews need to select materials assertively because, as Nilsen (1991) notes, "it's just harder to find the wheat because there's now twice as much chaff. . . . In today's climate, it's crucial that we become more assertive about measuring and communicating the quality of the books we've taken the time to read and evaluate" (pp. 181-182).

Because children's librarians are building a collection, they need to be told more than simply whether a book is or is not a good book. England and Fasick's checklist for evaluating books includes bibliographical information, authority of the author and publisher, audience, placing the book in context, illustrations, and physical format. For contemporary librarians, literary quality is not the sole determinant of purchasing decisions, and often it is not even the major determinant. Perhaps the most valuable part of a review is the information that places the book in context. How does this work compare with others in the same genre or on the same subject? Is this book a necessary purchase? In what type of collection would it be of value? Librarians are not just buying books; they are buying books to serve readers. They need specific information about how the book might be used by readers and how it can be used in their own work with children. Can it be used in preschool story hour? Will it be good for booktalking? Will it help students with school research? These qualities may give a book the extra value that determines whether or not to purchase it.

Although fewer than half the librarians in one survey (45%) use reviews in journals to select and defend acquisitions (Roback, 1991, p. 38), those who do use reviews use them to evaluate existing collections, to help establish a core collection, to serve as a jury of opinion and a forum for discussion, to defend their purchases, and to help them express their needs to publishers. To help them evaluate their collections, librarians use recommended and notable lists in reviewing journals, and they use book evaluation resources such as the *Children's Catalog* to help find the best materials possible. Since many librarians disagree about what children will find valuable, "reviews act as a jury of opinion" (England & Fasick, 1987, p. 23). Reviews have become a forum for discussing what makes a good children's book, and they have also become a vehicle for continuing education. Librarians discuss book reviews with each other and often rely on them to select books in areas where they have "no personal interest. . . . Librarians read and select from reviews so that when a library patron asks 'Do you have a (good) book about . . . ?' we can answer affirmatively. Helping us answer that question is the first function of reviews" (Sutton, 1986, p. 50).

Reviews also help librarians defend their choices. Unfortunately, the right of access to information is still sometimes denied to children. When children's librarians are asked to remove books from their collections, one of their many lines of defense is to show the professional evaluations and responses to the material being questioned. They can let reviews serve as witnesses for the defense.

Finally, reviews are a means for librarians, as consumers, to address the glut of children's materials. As Hammill (1990) writes,

> we can't expect the problems of oversupply to be solved by its source. As with most complex conditions (both the causes and the effects of too-many-new-children's-books are a tangle of finance, morality, aesthetics, education), there isn't a single remedy. Part of the answer, with hardbacks anyway, may lie in selectivity: publishing output could be refined, and quality improved, if professional book buyers—librarians and teachers, primarily—and their colleagues the reviewers were more coherent in what they bought and praised.
>
> Though self-evident, this remark has the virtue of emphasizing an inescapable equation: *buying* = *supporting*. . . . One way to begin to sort out the assumptions that underlie selecting books is to answer the question: "What are you giving children when you give them this book?" (p. 3)

That is why it is so important for reviews to say not simply whether a book is good but also how it compares to other books and exactly what collection needs it serves.

CRITICISM OF REVIEWS

Researchers have identified a number of things librarians criticize in reviews. Moreover, an informal series of interviews with children's librarians from a variety of libraries (Alpha Park Public Library District, Bartonville, IL; Arlington Heights Public Library, IL; Bensenville Public Library, IL; Clearwater Public Library System, FL; Harold Washington Public Library, Chicago, IL; Minneapolis Public Library and Information Center, MN; Monroe County Public Library,

Bloomington, IN; Normal Public Library, IL; Phoenix Public Library, AZ; St. Louis Public Library, MO; Urbana Free Library, IL) to learn what review journals they use, their selection process, and how they think journals could make reviews more useful, suggests that there has been some improvement since Goldberger's study of the inadequacies in review literature, but many of her findings are still pertinent (Sutherland, 1975, p. 23):

- inadequate reviewing of foreign language books;
- not enough reviews of new books about minority groups—especially Spanish surname, American Indian, and European-American ethnic groups;
- scanty reviewing of books from new or alternative presses;
- too few reviews of books considered for their potential use by the visually handicapped;
- not enough identification of high-interest, low-reading level books;
- too few suggestions for and too little comment on use of books in the home;
- the time lag between the publication of books and the appearance of reviews.

Reviews are often faulted as well for unreliable judgments, for summarizing the content rather than evaluating the quality, for excessive bias, and for using unqualified reviewers or reviewers who address the needs of their own libraries but not the needs of libraries at large. Moreover, nonfiction does not get reviewed as much as fiction:

> Titles from small specialized presses or from presses which do not send review copies to journals, have little chance of being picked for review. Ephemeral titles or titles that are considered a waste of children's time are not often chosen for review. Publishers' series books ... (romances, mysteries, participation books), are in this category. Yet, children are very interested in precisely these kinds of books. While many librarians agree that individual titles within a fiction series can have merit, it is difficult for any series book, including nonfiction series, to break into the circle of consistent, serious reviewing. (England & Fasick, 1987, p. 27)

The conclusions of these researchers are complemented and extended by some additional findings from my interviews with librarians. The librarians spoken with shared a number of the concerns already addressed. Some reviews are too biased, and librarians need more objective reviewing. Plot summaries or the effort merely to sound interesting can displace the information librarians need to help them decide whether to make a purchase. Cute verbosity gets substituted for clarity and conciseness. Ephemeral materials and books from small presses do not receive enough reviews or the same quality of reviews as books from established presses. The librarians also mentioned a number of other issues:

- Reviewers seem out of touch with actual librarians and their needs. They focus on literary quality rather than on what will appeal to children.
- Misinformation in reviews costs irreplaceable money. One librarian regretted purchasing multiple copies of a favorably reviewed book on sex that turned out to imply that children can protect themselves from AIDS by washing their hands.
- Reviews need to focus more on how the materials can be used.
- Reviews need to describe the book's format. Is the book an odd size? Will the binding last? Is it bound in an unusual way? Does it have inserts?
- Is the book unique? Is there something about it that no other book can provide?
- Some journals seem to expect all reviews to be favorable and make the book sound good. Reviews need to be more discriminating. Even if many of the books are good, which are the best ones to purchase? It would be refreshing for more reviews to say that items do *not* need to be purchased.
- Not enough reviews target the actual groups that real librarians serve.
- Although *VOYA* (*Voice of Youth Advocates*) covers young adult materials widely, other journals review them inadequately.
- Not enough reviews address series as series.
- Audiovisual materials and software do not receive the same quality reviewing as print.
- Not enough reviews cover materials about basic skills, for example, how to write a letter or how to fill out job applications.
- Reviews could say how one item compares to another. Do you need to get z if you already have x and y? Comparisons should address illustrations as well as text. If a reviewer says that the illustrations are like those in another book, it helps librarians visualize and evaluate it.
- When journals highlight controversial titles, they might provide three different reviews so that librarians can compare varying perspectives.
- One librarian mentioned that she would like nonfiction to be reviewed the way *Appraisal* reviews science titles, with one review from a science-expert and another from a librarian.
- Reviews would be even more useful if they were available online, which would also allow librarians to call up reviews through subject searches and compare various reviews before buying.

REVIEWS AND SELECTION

The interviews also revealed striking differences in the ways libraries select the materials they purchase. At some libraries, even large libraries, one librarian reads the review journals and makes all the purchasing decisions. At other libraries, the reading of reviews and the purchasing decisions are divided up among a group or committee of librarians. Committees might consist of librarians who represent different branches and different specialties. Some large- or medium-sized libraries distribute responsibility for different areas to each librarian. One person might cover one or more categories such as general nonfiction, audiovisual materials, fiction, or a particular subject area, and so on. At one library, each librarian has one or two areas, while all the librarians cover fiction. Some libraries order *School Library Journal* reviews-on-cards and make notes on them as they read additional reviews. Along with reviews, certain libraries use publishers' catalogs, selection services, and nonlibrary resources such as the *Journal of the Association for the Education of Young Children* and ERIC bibliographies. At another library, each librarian receives a certain dollar amount to spend each week, and they all rotate the responsibility for weekly book orders. A number of libraries receive books on approval. A larger library with many branches receives preview copies of almost all the children's books published in a given year. The librarians can read or examine the actual books as they read the reviews. Many libraries use reviews to assemble multicultural bibliographies and booklists for summer reading clubs or to select titles for booktalking.

Altogether, children's librarians use reviews in a wide variety of ways and need to do a better job of informing review journals about their needs. Librarians make their best use of reviews when they read them in light of the ongoing demands of a collection development policy. When they read the review of a particular book, therefore, they have more to consider than the isolated value of that particular book. They must also consider how the review can help define the value of that book for that particular library. Reading reviews should not be a passive process, where librarians check off which book is good and which is bad. A librarian can measure what each book offers against his or her library's continuing needs and against the existing collection and the circulation history of similar books. Librarians do not let reviews make their decisions for them. Instead, they use reviews to help them make their own decisions. Reviews may reflect the limits of technology and culture, but librarians also describe them as a helpful resource that provides an invaluable service.

REFERENCES

Cummins, J. (1989). Design of youth services. In L. Edmonds (Ed.), *Managers and missionaries: Library services to children and young adults in the information age*

(Papers presented at the 28th Allerton Park Institute, 14-16 November 1986) (pp. 29-40). Urbana-Champaign: University of Illinois, Graduate School of Library and Information Science.

Eberhart, G. M. (1991). *The whole library handbook: Current data, professional advice, and curiosa about libraries and library service.* Chicago, IL: American Library Association.

England, C., & Fasick, A. M. (1987). *Childview: Evaluating and reviewing materials for children.* Littleton, CO: Libraries Unlimited.

Gorman, G. E., & Howes, B. R. (1989). *Collection development for libraries.* London: Bowker-Saur.

Hammill, E. (1990). Introduction. In N. Chambers (Ed.), *The Signal selection of children's books, 1989.* Oxford: Thimble Press.

Huck, C. S.; Hepler, S.; & Hickman, J. (1987). *Children's literature in the elementary school* (4th ed.). New York: Holt, Rinehart, and Winston.

Huntoon, E. (1992, June). *Children's librarians: The keybrokers of childhood.* Paper presented at the annual conference of the American Library Association, San Francisco, CA.

Nilsen, A. P. (1991). Speaking loudly for good books: Promoting the wheat & winnowing the chaff. *School Library Journal, 37*(9), 181-182.

Roback, D. (1991, May 31). Checking out children's books. *Publishers Weekly,* pp. 38-39.

Simora, F. (1991). *The Bowker annual: Library and book trade almanac* (36th ed.). New Providence, NJ: R. R. Bowker.

Smith, C. B. (1989). Trends in teaching reading. *Reading Teacher, 42*(9), 720.

Sutherland, Z. B. (1975). Book reviews: Before and after. *School Library Journal, 21*(6), 22-23.

Sutton, R. (1986). Reviewing Avi. *School Library Journal, 32*(9), 50.

Trelease, J. (1985). *The read-aloud handbook.* New York: Penguin Books.

Walters, V. A. (1992). *Output measures for public library service to children: A manual of standardized procedures.* Chicago, IL: American Library Association.

JANIE SCHOMBERG

School Library Media Specialist
Leal Elementary School
Urbana, Illinois

Tools of the Trade:
School Library Media Specialists,
Reviews, and Collection Development

INTRODUCTION

How many times might you peer into a school library media center in a school building in the United States and see this picture? A school library media specialist sits at a library table in a darkened building late in the afternoon looking at what seems to be an oversized, overwhelming jigsaw puzzle. Six thousand of the pieces represent the approximate number of children's books published annually, 4,000 small pieces represent the number of dollars allotted to purchase books for the year, and 500 pieces of more prominent size and shape represent the number of students and staff served by the school library media collection. Off to the side of the table is a small box into which all the puzzle pieces must fit, representing the average cost of children's books, now hovering near the $15 mark. Did you recognize me at the table? Although the number of pieces may vary greatly, this puzzle is a visual image of the collection development dilemma faced by all school library media specialists every year.

COLLECTION DEVELOPMENT

Information Power: Guidelines for School Library Media Programs (American Association of School Librarians [AASL], 1988) states that "collection development is a systematic process administered by the library media staff to bring together the materials and equipment to meet users' needs" (p. 72). This definition could apply to any type of library. Is there anything truly unique to collection development in the public school setting? What are the guidelines and procedures for a school library media specialist to examine and implement in order to develop and manage a collection effectively?

In Illinois, four primary factors in the school culture determine the context for the selection of materials for the school library media collection. First, all public schools in Illinois are required to adhere to the State Goals for Learning that have been established in the areas of the social sciences, biological and physical sciences, mathematics, language arts, physical development and health, and fine arts. In addition to these goals, certain topics are mandated to be taught, among these being African-American history, women's history, and the Holocaust. Also to be considered at the state level are the *Illinois School Library Media Program Guidelines* (Illinois Library Association [ILA], 1992), which include a major section on resources and equipment. Our broad goals and guidelines in the public schools are, therefore, predetermined at the state level.

At the school district level, the local learning outcomes are based upon the State Goals. These outcomes must be developed for each curriculum content area. Specific to materials, a local school district is encouraged to formulate a collection development plan which, according to *Information Power* (AASL, 1988),

> provides a broad overview of the needs and priorities of the school's collection, based on the short- and long-range goals of the library media program and on an assessment of the strengths and weaknesses of the collection, and provides specific guidelines for building and maintaining the school's collection. (p. 75)

School districts are more likely to have a districtwide selection policy that addresses only some of the components articulated in the *Information Power* collection development definition, specifically the selection and acquisition of materials.

The third factor is the community in which the school is located and the geographical areas from which the students come, whether they are one and the same or distinctly different. An understanding of the demographics of the clientele is a critical factor in the collection development process.

The fourth and final factor is the building culture, which includes such things as the way the building is organized and the teaching and learning styles that are part of that local school. The building in which I am the school library media specialist differs greatly from individual buildings in other districts and somewhat from the other buildings in the Urbana school district.

My particular building culture is Leal School, a K-5 elementary school with 457 students, which serves the local neighborhood as well as several other neighborhoods that are not contiguous. Leal serves an economically diverse population as well as a culturally diverse one. While the Urbana school district curriculum provides a skeletal framework of learning outcomes, each building determines the specific nature of what is taught in order to accomplish those outcomes.

The Leal Alternatives Program was developed and implemented to provide three environmental variations within one school, all consistent with the school philosophy and designed to meet the needs of our students. Kindergarten is a full-day, self-contained classroom instructional setting, while in grades 1-4, a choice of instructional styles is offered, including a team-teaching environment of grades 1-2 or 3-4, a primarily self-contained environment of 1-2 or 3-4, or a single-grade classroom of 1, 2, 3, or 4. Students in grades 1-4 stay with the same teacher for two years in all environment choices. These classrooms offer an alternative-year curriculum, covering the learning outcomes and content for two grades over a two-year period.

Fifth grade is composed of a three-teacher team that departmentalizes instruction in major content areas. All choices and configurations strive to integrate the disciplines in a curriculum subscribing to a whole-language philosophy. Throughout Leal School, there are no textbooks—all teaching and learning is resource based. This philosophy and teaching style place the focus of curriculum support on the school library media center requiring a very different collection development process than, for instance, a school that has required textbooks throughout the district and a lock-step curriculum.

My collection development plan is always evolving. Perhaps you have heard all you ever want to hear about trickle-down theories, but my guess is that you have not heard about the trickle-down collection development plan. Leal School is a building showing its age and lacking the attention of a regular preventive maintenance program. Last November on a dreary Saturday afternoon, I received a call from one of the library staff indicating that there was a major problem at school and asking me to come over as soon as possible. What I encountered was four inches of hot water all over the floor of the library media center and one entire shelf area and assorted other nooks and crannies that had been soaked with clean, almost boiling water from the bursting of a ceiling water pipe. The irony of the situation was that the major section obliterated by the "flood" was the weather section with the book entitled *It's Raining Cats and Dogs* a sample of the worst damage to an individual title. We were sad, mad, and many other things but went about the work of assessing the damage and replacing the hundreds of lost items—both print and nonprint.

You've heard that lightning never strikes in the same place twice—wrong! In mid-January, the pipe on the other side of the library media center burst in exactly the same way while I was assisting a class of primary-grade children to find materials. Because we were there when that pipe burst, we were able to minimize the damage but lost the majority of our pets section. In response to these mini-disasters, I proposed a new plan to my principal—the revolving collection development plan. I suggested that if I rotated the entire collection every month, changing the location of major sections, we might eventually be able to replace all the books should our pipes stage repeat performances!

While various general forces—including, obviously, natural disasters—determine the school culture, there are more specific factors affecting school library media collections. Economic factors are the first to come to mind, affecting the monies school districts get from the state and the monies that are then designated by the local district for support of school library media collections. *School Library Journal* provides annual statistics on budget support for school library media centers. The average book budget of a school library media center is approximately one-fourth of the average book budget for a public library children's department (Roback, 1991, p. 38). Of course, the state of the economy in general is an external factor that affects us all.

The commercial market also affects our choices and options. What are the "hot topics" of the moment that are so readily available on the market? How much are we at the mercy of the publishing industry and book jobbers in our selection of materials? What percentage must we overorder to fulfill our orders? What about those out-of-print problems?

Social factors impinge upon school and public libraries in untold ways. Demographics are constantly changing as we survey and assess our clientele. The mobility of school populations is incredible. The number of at-risk students seems to be ever increasing. Our roles as caretakers seem to increase daily as schools are expected to offer social services. Cultural diversity is a growing challenge as we try to effectively teach and learn from many cultures and life-styles.

Technology is allowing us to expand our horizons. Depending upon the range of our technological capabilities, we can offer more services and resources as well as increase our field of networking and cooperation.

MATERIALS SELECTION

Bearing in mind that these school culture and external factors set the scene for my selection process, just exactly how do I go about selecting materials for the Leal Library? Having been there for only two full years, after serving a school district in Minnesota for 18 years, I am still struggling to get a handle on the curriculum. The fluid structure of the district curriculum and the autonomy granted individual teachers in my building make that a full-time challenge complicated by our two-year curriculum cycle at Leal.

One of the keys to becoming informed about the curriculum is involving the teachers in the process. The staff at Leal is a group of very dedicated, knowledgeable teachers who know and care a great deal about teaching/learning materials. They are continually on the lookout for potential library materials through their own involvement in conferences, workshops, coursework, and constant use of the two public libraries that serve our communities, and they are bookstore fanatics. The teachers at Leal recommend materials to me on a regular basis through informal verbal exchanges as well as more formal recommendation forms and requests. The professional review journals that are subscribed to through the school library media center are also routed, by request, to many teachers in the building who regularly read and mark reviews for my consideration.

My personal/professional selection process is based primarily on the use of reviews but is augmented on occasion by the serendipitous means of directly examining books via conferences, workshops, public libraries, vendor contacts, and frequent bookstore perusal. How do book reviews fit into my selection process? After I have assessed my school population, carefully examined the curriculum, and determined the needs and priorities of the collection, I rely on book reviews to form the core of information and opinion for my materials selection.

BOOK REVIEWS AND MATERIALS SELECTION

I need and expect a lot from book reviews. First, book reviews should be descriptive, objective statements about plot, characters, theme, and illustrations. Second, I expect book reviews to have an evaluative statement including comparison of the title being reviewed to similar titles and literature in general. Third, the potential appeal, curricular use, and possible controversial aspects of the title need to be addressed to fully inform me as a potential selector. Using sound reviewing resources and selection procedures assists librarians in developing documentation/rationale in the event of a request for reconsideration of an item or title (Reichman, 1988).

Book reviews certainly do not meet all our needs. First, there are limited reviews of specialized materials. School library media specialists are most often confined to general selection tools and journals and may not have access to journals that provide specialized reviews. Second, some reviews and reviewing sources have a rather "generic" quality and vocabulary and therefore may not be as reliable as others. Third, there may be a significant time lag between the publication of the item and the review of same. This is less of a problem for school library media specialists than for public librarians, as our budgets are rather limited and ordering is usually done only two to three times a year. Fourth, there seems to be no way to avoid the occasional "lemon."

My favorite "lemon" story is a personal one. Over 20 years ago when my husband and I were preparing to purchase our first home, we combed the want ads early each Sunday morning searching for a house that would fit our needs and our budget. One such morning, I was reading along and immediately got excited about the house described. It sounded like the perfect house for us in a great location at a price toward the top end of our limits. It wasn't until I read completely to the end of the advertisement that I realized the house being described was the less-than-perfect rental house in which we were currently living! I always think back to that experience when I receive a title that may have struck one person's fancy or met one curricular need but is definitely off-base for the collection in the library media center in the building I serve. Selection of materials based upon reviews cannot be expected to be successful 100% of the time!

As the person responsible for the selection and purchase of materials for a school library media center, I employ a broad range of reviewing sources and approaches. Reviews by professional reviewers have a different flavor and focus than those by field reviewers. Both perspectives are essential to making informed decisions. We all need to make more of an effort to address multicultural issues in the review and selection of materials. In building multicultural-multilingual collections, we need to be ever mindful of the general criteria for selection in addition to giving consideration to the more specific concerns of authorship, content, language, characterization, theme, and physical format of multicultural materials (Jackson & Robertson, 1991, pp. 11-12).

Hamilton (1988) states, "It is very difficult to choose materials for a school library. To do the job properly, the teacher-librarian has to be **fully** aware of every curriculum thrust in the school, every teacher's teaching styles, every kid's reading level, every item in the existing collection" (p. 5). Can any of us truly do the job properly? Van Orden (1988) includes a comment from John Belland, in reporting on the results of a national survey:

> It is intriguing, then, to notice that both media program personnel and publishers/producer respondents ranked favorable reviews as being the most important selection factor. This would tend to imply that school personnel have neither the time nor the commitment to analyze materials in terms of a particular curricular need. They defer judgment to those persons who are professionally involved in reviewing a wide variety of materials. (p. 119)

Yes, I do depend upon book reviewers who work with a wide variety of materials to help me make informed decisions. However, I must come to those reviewing sources knowing the curricular needs of the staff and students as well as the strengths and weaknesses of the collection for which I am responsible. With those factors uppermost in my mind, my major selection criteria focus on the literary and artistic worth, the intellectual content, the age and ability appropriateness, and the overall value of the title or item in meeting the educational needs of my users.

When and where do I read these reviews and build my consideration file? It is a rare school library media specialist who is able to find quiet, uninterrupted time *or* space at work to devote to professional reading of any kind, particularly reviews, so most of us focus on selection in our homes. Review journals find their way to a stack on my desk at home waiting for quiet perusal there. I mark those titles I wish to add to my consideration file, which is kept up to date using FileMaker Pro on the Macintosh. Book orders are then built from my consideration file.

The most systematic and thorough process of selection that I have seen was a process employed by a Minnesota colleague several years ago. She methodically read reviews, copied the ones she wished to put in her consideration file, and transferred them to notecards. Careful consideration was only given to those titles for which she had copied and clipped a minimum of two and preferably three reviews. She then evaluated these titles/items very carefully in terms of the need and balance factor before making final selections. Selection was a high priority for her, and the quality of the collections for which she was responsible reflected that.

Let's take a closer look at how reviews helped me in the selection of three specific titles recently. First, *The Great Kapok Tree* by Lynne Cherry (1990). I examined four journals that reviewed this title upon publication. Reviewers agreed that the book was most appropriate for ages 4-8. The following are excerpted phrases that I found particularly helpful in my selection process. "Carefully researched," "endpaper map" (Corsaro, 1990, p. 1443), "stunning endpapers" (Jenks, 1990, p. 321), and "attractive environmental brief" (Long, 1990, p. 177) helped me know that the title would probably be effective in our curricular areas of social studies and science focusing on the rain forest. "Large format" (Corsaro, 1990, p. 1443) indicated that the title could be used with small and large groups, while "simple and clear" and "rich colored-pencil and watercolor drawings" (Toth, 1990, p. 82) gave me a good sense of the visual and verbal aspects of this title. "Story is heavy-handed" (Jenks,

1990, p. 321) and "thinly veiled nature and conservation lesson" (Toth, 1990, p. 82) helped me know that the book would need to be used with other similar titles in order to provide balance.

A title about the Holocaust (one of our state-mandated topics), *The Lily Cupboard* by Shulamith Oppenheim (1992), generated at least six reviews. Reviewers generally agreed that this title is appropriate for ages 5-10. This is a sensitive subject and one for which I continue to look for titles that are suitable for primary-graders. The reviews helped me determine such suitability: "gentle story" (Zeiger, 1992, p. 193), "exceptionally sensitive and effective portrayal of a difficult subject" (Long, 1991, p. 1596), "realistically childlike focus," "a picture book simultaneously gentle and sharp in its perspective on the Holocaust" (Hearne, 1992a, p. 190), "rich watercolor and gouache paintings" (Abbott, 1992, p. 953), "used . . . in a classroom setting or by parents, this could provide a memorable introduction to the suffering and bravery of individuals during the war" (Sherman, 1992, p. 97). Did I feel like I was making an informed selection? Yes!

Selecting resources that will be of particular interest to teachers is a high priority for school library media specialists. *Talking with Artists* edited by Pat Cummings (1992) is just such a book, and I selected it for Leal Library this year. Reviews in five journals agreed that this is an exceptional book that could be enjoyed and used by readers of all ages beginning with third grade. Such phrases as "innovative approach to informational books" (Burns, 1992, p. 465), "beautifully reproduced samples of current work" (Wilton, 1992, p. S28), "candidly child-like questions" (Hearne, 1992b, p. 202) "delight for aspiring artists" (Zvirin, 1992, p. 1598), "represent a range of styles and interests," and "minority, girl, and economically deprived readers can find role models among the fourteen artists" (Hoyle, 1992, p. 62) convinced me that this was an essential title for the Leal Library.

CONCLUSION

In fulfilling the three roles of today's school library media specialist, those of information specialist, teacher, and instructional partner, the selection of materials must be a high priority. If quality materials are not available and accessible in and through the school library media center, the effectiveness of all three roles will be greatly diminished. Our mission to "facilitate students and teachers becoming effective users of ideas and information" (ILA, 1988, p. 1) will not be met.

Book reviews are essential tools in building a collection, our link as "solo" librarians to what is being published. Members of a skilled trade carefully select the right tool only after they have analyzed the task at hand. Should we as school library media specialists be expected to do any less? We must make it a high priority to analyze and plan for our task, sound collection development, and then skillfully, not willfully, use the tools that will help us select materials "to support the school's curriculum and to contribute to the learning goals of teachers and students" (AASL, 1988, p. 82).

REFERENCES

Abbott, D. (1992). Review of *The lily cupboard* by S. L. Oppenheim. *Booklist, 88*(10), 953.

American Association of School Librarians and Association for Educational Communications and Technology. (1988). *Information power: Guidelines for school library media programs.* Chicago, IL: American Library Association; Washington, DC: AECT.

Burns, M. M. (1992). Review of *Talking with artists* by P. Cummings. *Horn Book Magazine, 68*(4), 465-466.

Cherry, L. (1990). *The great kapok tree: A tale of the Amazon rain forest.* San Diego, CA: Harcourt Brace Jovanovich.

Corsaro, J. (1990). Review of *The great kapok tree: A tale of the Amazon rain forest* by L. Cherry. *Booklist, 86*(14), 1443.

Cummings, P. (Comp. & Ed.). (1992). *Talking with artists.* New York: Bradbury.

Hamilton, D. (1988). The other hand. *School Libraries in Canada, 8*(3), 5-6.

Hearne, B. (1992a). Review of *The lily cupboard* by S. L. Oppenheim. *Bulletin of the Center for Children's Books, 45*(7), 190.

Hearne, B. (1992b). Review of *Talking with artists* by P. Cummings. *Bulletin of the Center for Children's Books, 45*(8), 202.

Hoyle, K. N. (1992). Review of *Talking with artists* by P. Cummings. *Five Owls, 6*(5), 62-63.

Illinois Library Association and Illinois School Library Media Association Guidelines Writing Committee. (1992). *Illinois school library media program guidelines.* Chicago, IL: ILA.

Jackson, G., & Robertson, M. (1991). Building multicultural-multilingual collections. *CMLEA Journal: Official Publication of the California Media and Library Educators Association, 15*(1), 11-13.

Jenks, C. K. (1990). Review of *The great kapok tree: A tale of the Amazon rain forest* by L. Cherry. *Horn Book Magazine, 66*(2), 321.

Long, J. R. (Ed.). (1990). Review of *The great kapok tree: A tale of the Amazon rain forest* by L. Cherry. *Kirkus Reviews, 58*(3), 177.

Long, J. R. (Ed.). (1991). Review of *The lily cupboard* by S. L. Oppenheim. *Kirkus Reviews, 59*(24), 1596.

McDonald, M. (1992). Review of *The lily cupboard* by S. L. Oppenheim. *Five Owls, 6*(4), 78.

Oppenheim, S. L. (1992). *The lily cupboard.* Illustrated by R. Himler. New York: HarperCollins.

Reichman, H. (1988). *Censorship and selection: Issues and answers for schools.* Chicago, IL: American Library Association; Arlington, VA: American Association of School Administration.

Roback, D. (1991, May 31). Checking out children's books. *Publishers Weekly*, pp. 38-39.

Sherman, L. L. (1992). Review of *The lily cupboard* by S. L. Oppenheim. *School Library Journal, 38*(4), 97.

Toth, L. (1990). Review of *The great kapok tree: A tale of the Amazon rain forest* by L. Cherry. *School Library Journal, 36*(5), 82.

Van Orden, P. J. (1988). *The collection program in schools: Concepts, practices, and information sources.* Littleton, CO: Libraries Unlimited.

Wilton, S. (1992, June). Review of *Talking with artists* by P. Cummings. *School Library Journal* (Supplement), pp. S28-S29.

Zeiger, H. B. (1992). Review of *The lily cupboard* by S. L. Oppenheim. *Horn Book Magazine, 68*(2), 193.

Zvirin, S. (1992). Review of *Talking with artists* by P. Cummings. *Booklist, 88*(17), 1598.

VIOLET HARRIS

Associate Professor
Curriculum and Instruction
University of Illinois at Urbana-Champaign

Evaluating Children's Books for Whole-Language Learning

WHOLE LANGUAGE'S DEFINING CHARACTERISTICS

Whole language is a philosophy, perspective, world view, or stance; it is not a program of hierarchical components or methods (Blake, 1990; Teale, 1992; K. S. Goodman, 1986, 1990, 1992; Hoffman, 1992). It is a grass roots movement spearheaded by teachers with empowerment of teachers and students as a central theme. Whole language is an amalgam of theories, beliefs, perspectives, and research about language, children, and learning drawn from a number of interrelated disciplines such as linguistics, psychology, philosophy, and sociology. Further, whole language is the perspective that learning occurs when information is presented as a whole rather than divided into smaller components and is thus meaningful; activities occur within a social context, and the learner is active. Kenneth Goodman, a major proponent of whole language whom many consider a founding father, identified its key features (K. S. Goodman, 1986, pp. 38-40):

Principles for Reading and Writing

- Readers construct meaning during reading. They use their prior learning and experience to make sense of the texts.
- Readers predict, select, confirm, and self-correct as they seek to make sense of print.
- Writers include enough information and detail so what they write will be comprehensible to their readers.

- Three language systems interact in written language: the graphophonic, the syntactic, and the semantic.
- Comprehension of meaning is always the goal of readers.
- Expression of meaning is always what writers are trying to achieve.
- Writers and readers are strongly limited by what they already know, writers in composing, readers in comprehending.

People also enquire about what makes whole language whole. Kenneth Goodman (1986, p. 40) identified those features as well:

- Whole-language learning builds around whole learners learning whole language in whole situations.
- Whole-language learning assumes respect for language, for the learner, and for the teacher.
- The focus is on meaning and not on language itself, in authentic speech and literacy events.
- Learners are encouraged to take risks and invited to use language, in all its varieties, for their own purposes.
- In a whole-language classroom, all the varied functions of oral and written language are appropriate and encouraged.

THE WHOLE-LANGUAGE CLASSROOM

Application of these principles results in a radically different kind of classroom. Teachers and students take power; they share jointly in decision making, and they negotiate some aspects of the curriculum. Publishers, test makers, and consultants are not the arbiters of curricula. Teachers shed their role as "de-skilled" technicians and assume the role of a professional, a facilitator who guides learning. They assume responsibility (accountability) for what occurs in the classrooms. Students are active seekers of knowledge. They understand that they possess the ability to acquire the strategies needed to learn. Parents, too, assume a more integral role. The learning that takes place in the school is connected to the homes and communities in which students reside. Family and community members are encouraged to participate and share their knowledge and expertise with students. Their participation is not limited to homework checks or open houses.

What might a whole-language classroom look like to the visitor? Some characteristics are universal, others individual (Blake, 1990; Teale, 1992; K. S. Goodman, 1986, 1990; Hydrick & Wildermuth, 1990). First, the visitor would notice that the noise level fluctuates; whole-language classrooms are not silent. Talk is an integral feature.

Second, the physical layout of the room differs from the tradition of permanently anchored desks and seats. Whole-language classrooms feature learning centers for math, writing, art, music, science, social studies, and reading. Books, magazines, newspapers, and other print materials such as maps, pamphlets, recipes, etc., abound. Basal readers are absent. Listening stations with tape recorders and audio materials are prominent. Children's writing, art, and other projects receive center stage. Seating is structured in small clusters. The teacher's desk is not the center of the classroom.

Third, "lessons" are active and varied. For instance, rather than three reading groups, a teacher uses heterogeneous groupings that change across task and subject. The teacher might structure four or more groups to discuss a book, complete paired reading, dramatize a section of a book, read additional information about an author or illustrator, or create a visual representation of a passage.

Fourth, evaluation is continuous and completed in order to guide learners, identify and celebrate their strengths, and discover areas that require additional work. Portfolios containing examples of students' work are the norm, rather than standardized tests.

Fifth, content subject matter is integrated. There are no unconnected periods for reading, spelling, and writing. Language crosses all subject matters, and all subject matter is connected.

The teacher in a whole-language classroom is a reader and a writer. She reads and writes about a variety of genres and topics. She knows children's literature; if not, she is informed enough to know that various review journals and guides exist that will provide information. The teacher shares her experiences as a writer and reader with her students. In the process, she shares her enthusiasm and models strategies that are effective for each mode of discourse. In addition, she develops and uses a professional library of essential texts on whole language such as those written by the Goodmans, Nancy Atwell, Donald Graves, Don Holdaway, Lucy Calkins, and others. She also reads other professional literature for insights into language and learning.

Most importantly, the teacher adopts a new attitude relative to her power in the classroom. She is no longer the sole source of knowledge. She develops within her students the belief that they, too, are sources of knowledge. She negotiates with her students. This does not mean, however, that she relinquishes all decision making. Rather, it means that she offers her students options. Perhaps they would prefer to work individually rather than in small groups to create some dialogue. The teacher becomes a "kid-watcher" (Y. M. Goodman, 1985). Kid-watching helps her monitor students' progress and their interactions with others so that she can make informed curricula decisions. She conducts her classroom in such a manner that students are active learners who learn meaningful information that connects with their lives inside and outside of school.

THE WHOLE-LANGUAGE DEBATE

Advocates of whole language argue that this type of classroom and teacher are possible at all levels of schooling. Critics contend that the whole-language classroom is without direction and structure, that children slip through the cracks if they are not average or above average in performance. Also, some consider the movement elitist and not applicable to urban school districts or school systems with limited English proficient (LEP) or bilingual students.

Some criticize what they perceive as a smug intolerance on the part of whole-language advocates (Hoffman, 1992). Those who do not adopt a whole-language stance are made to feel as if they are pariahs and harmful to children. Numerous articles in the *Reading Teacher* and *Language Arts* convey this sentiment directly and indirectly. Leaders in this grass roots movement can alienate as well. For instance, Kenneth Goodman (1992) lambasts Marilyn Adams (1990) and her book, *Beginning to Read: Thinking and Learning about Print,* and the Center for the Study of Reading (CSR), particularly those responsible for creating a 150-page summary of Adams' book, for their alleged duplicity in buckling under to the "far right" policy makers in the Department of Education. According to Goodman, Department of Education officials threatened to decrease or eliminate funding for the CSR unless it produced a report stating that phonics instruction was crucial in early literacy experiences.

Others accuse whole-language advocates of controlling periodicals devoted to literacy issues (Groff, 1992). Groff wrote the editors of the *Reading Teacher* to determine whether the *Reading Teacher* had relinquished its neutral stance regarding literacy instruction in order to "extravagantly" favor whole language. According to Groff, the *Reading Teacher,* from 1986-1991, published 115 articles that extolled whole language. The editors responded that they published only 10-15% of manuscripts submitted that related to whole language or literature-based reading instruction.

Delpit (1986, 1988) created extensive debate when she argued that whole language was at odds with the instructional practices of many African-American teachers and the expectations of African-American students. She found that many of her colleagues were more directive and emphasized skills. Consequently, Delpit argued, their students gained access to valuable cultural knowledge. Delpit did not suggest that African-American students did not need whole language but rather that factors such as race/ethnicity, historical experiences, interactive styles, and access to cultural knowledge influenced the effectiveness of any method or perspective. Other researchers working with Asian/ Pacific Islander and Latino/a students concurred with some of Delpit's criticism (Au, 1980; Wong Fillmore & Valadez, 1986).

Ladson-Billings (1992), in contrast, observed and interviewed teachers deemed effective in their efforts with African-American students. She found that effective teachers incorporated the realities of the sociopolitical milieu. They practiced a "culturally relevant" style of teaching, one that empowered students "intellectually, socially, emotionally, and politically by using cultural referents to impart knowledge, skills, and attitudes" (p. 382). These salient features paralleled those that should appear in whole-language classrooms; however, whole-language proponents were usually silent on issues of race, class, and gender or touched upon them in tangential fashion. Ladson-Billings and other advocates of critical pedagogy provide convincing evidence that literacy and access to knowledge are essential components of cultural hegemony and that becoming literate in whole language or other classes is an overtly political action.

Another criticism of whole language relates to the perceived lack of an explicit curriculum. Critics contend that anything goes in whole-language classrooms, that students learn in a hit-or-miss fashion, and that the philosophy is best suited for average and above average students (K. S. Goodman, 1992). Further, critics such as E. D. Hirsch (1987) argued that there exists a body of knowledge reflecting the cumulative heritage of the nation, its histories, and the values advocated by citizens and that students should acquire this knowledge. Others such as Chall (1983) argued for some phonics in the literacy curriculum because meta-analyses of research completed within the past 30 years revealed that some instruction in phonics is crucial for learning to read. Whole-language advocates counter these arguments by stating that predetermined curricula violate an essential tenet of students' determining some of the knowledge they are to learn. Also, they argue that sound-symbol relationships should be taught within the context of whole, meaningful print.

A final criticism of whole language revolves around the collection of data that documents its effectiveness. Critics state that studies lack methodological rigor, that the musings of teachers in journals do not constitute objective evidence. Proponents counter by stating that whole language lends itself more to qualitative research methods, with multiple data sources such as content analysis, audio- and visual-recordings, observation notes, journal entries, interviews, and samples of students' work (Hydrick & Wildermuth, 1990).

Whole-language advocates proclaim that the movement has swept the nation and has become entrenched (K. S. Goodman, 1986; Hydrick & Wildermuth, 1990). Cullinan (1992) concurs with this belief. Her research revealed that only 9 states had statewide initiatives focusing on literature, 16 had initiatives centered on integrated language arts, and 22 did not have any statewide initiatives, but that at a grass roots level, individual districts, schools, and teachers had adopted the perspective. Despite these claims, many teachers approach literacy by including phonics instruction and sharing literature with students occasionally; most are not whole-language teachers (Langer, Applebee, Mullis, & Foertsch, 1990).

Whole language will not disappear. It has gained a tremendous foothold in the two major literacy organizations, the International Reading Association and the National Council of Teachers of English. Both organizations sponsor pre- and post-convention institutes, workshops, and symposia on the topic. At both conferences, a "day of whole language" is an expected feature, attracting several hundreds to over a thousand teachers. Whole language has also become institutionalized. Professors who advocate the perspective are found in major colleges and universities preparing a new generation of teachers. What then, are the evaluative criteria that should guide the selection of literature in whole-language classes?

SELECTING LITERATURE FOR WHOLE LANGUAGE

Undoubtedly, basal readers are the one type of written material universally banned in whole-language classrooms. In fact, teachers are admonished to throw out the basal as the first step. Kenneth Goodman (1988) popularized the term "basalization of children's literature" to describe the manner in which publishers rewrite literary texts to conform to readability formulas, change gender and ethnicities of characters, truncate syntax, and control vocabulary. Silvey (1989) also decried the basalization of children's literature in the form of literature guides that were often double the length of the trade book.

These are valid criticisms; however, one can make the argument that teachers might ban the basal prematurely. The late 1980s and 1990s signalled the renewed, or at least a newly acknowledged, emphasis of cultural diversity or multiculturalism in children's literature. Publishers of trade books did not respond as quickly as publishers of basal programs. For example, Lindgren (1991) reported that only 51 books published in 1990 included African-Americans; far fewer books about Latinos/as, Asian/Pacific Islanders, and Native Americans were published. Meyer Reimer (1992) reported that basal readers were more expansive in their inclusions of multicultural literature. Evidence exists to support this contention. Scott Foreman's new program, Celebrate Reading!, is fully one-fourth multicultural in content. These facts suggest a need to retain basals for their cultural diversity, given the shrinking budgets of school and public libraries and the limited numbers of books reflecting cultural diversity that appear on the monthly best-seller lists compiled by *Publishers Weekly.* In 1990, 10 books about people of color appeared on the lists. Many of these, such as the "Indian" books of Lynn R. Banks, were controversial. Only two fit Rudine Sims Bishop's criteria of culturally conscious literature. Moreover, fewer than 10 have appeared on the lists for 1991 and 1992. One can argue that these data do not reflect school and public library purchases, but they offer insights on the kinds of books purchased by the public in bookstores.

Following the principles delineated by Kenneth Goodman (1986), the literature should reflect students' interests and tastes, the teacher's duty to guide and refine students' interests and tastes, and should engage them in meaningful ways. They should experience "real" literature. Rudine Sims Bishop (1990) provides an apt summary of what the literature should do:

> Books are sometimes windows, offering views of worlds that may be real or imagined, familiar or strange. These windows are also sliding glass doors, and readers have only to walk through in imagination to become part of whatever world has been created or recreated by the author. When lighting conditions are just right, however, a window can also be a mirror. Literature transforms human experience and reflects it back to us, and in that reflection we can see our own lives and experiences as part of the larger human experience. Reading, then, becomes a means of self affirmation, and readers often seek their mirrors in books. (p. ix)

In short, teachers should make available books that children would select for themselves, such as the Berenstain Bears, Teenage Mutant Ninja Turtles, Baby-Sitters Club, Sweet Valley High, Choose Your Own Adventure, romance series, and other books that entertain. Teachers are also responsible for introducing children to broader worlds and examples of literary excellence that provide models for writing, encourage critical thinking, and cause children to want to read more. Among the books included in this category would be traditional and contemporary classics such as *The Tale of Peter Rabbit, Treasure Island, Dear Mr. Henshaw, Bridge to Terabithia,* and *M. C. Higgins, the Great.* Teachers cannot select books on the basis of demographics. For example, you do not select *Abuela* (Dorros, 1991) just because you have Latino/a students; you select it because the folkloric motifs and the portrayal of the relationship between granddaughter and grandmother are well done or your students are interested in the story.

Specifically, books for preschool and primary children should contain repetitive phrases, rhythmic language, predictable text, and characters and events familiar to young children. The books should possess a structure that children can easily comprehend. Categories of literature that are important for this age group include poetry, folklore, nonfiction, wordless picture books, picture storybooks, and board books.

Children in intermediate, middle, and upper elementary grades require literature that "encourages confidence and risk-taking," and that helps improve strategies for reading and writing. The teacher's role is to help students expand their tastes and interests, acquire literary analysis skills, and promote the use of writing in functional contexts. Self-selection of reading material, as well as opportunities to share literature, is important. Appropriate literature at this juncture would include series fiction, award winners such as Newbery books, functional literacy materials, and nonfiction. In all cases, the teacher's selection of literature is guided by the needs of students in her classroom and is balanced against her responsibility to provide them essential, meaningful knowledge that enables them to understand themselves, family members, peers, community members, and other individuals with whom they may or may not have direct contact.

WHOLE LANGUAGE AND THE PUBLIC

Those involved with children's literature have achieved some successes. Messages about the importance of children's books were delivered; some people heard them and responded accordingly. For example, the number of children's-only bookstores increased to 450 in a little over a decade (Lodge, 1991). Sales approached $1^1/_2$ billion dollars, and best-sellers appeared periodically. A new education market emerged. Some of the improved distribution of children's literature is attributable to the spread of the whole-language movement. Much has been accomplished, but significantly more remains to be done. For purposes of promotion, children's literature and whole-language advocates can learn a lot from popular culture.

Popular culture provides insights in unexpected ways. It also demonstrates how educators could reach more people and provide them with essential knowledge about schooling. Consider, for example, the phenomenon of shopping by television as structured by the Home Shopping Network, the Fashion Channel, and QVC. Many in academe and other "highbrow" cultural institutions such as publishing scoff at the notion of watching these shows or purchasing merchandise through them. Television shopping is lowbrow, fodder for late-night comedians. However, one could argue that the shopping networks offer a window to the world of the "average" citizen. These average citizens focus on family, friends, home, and hearth. They seem patriotic, religious, and committed to the value of education as the great equalizer. Several million people tune in daily. The various hosts bond with the viewers and seem genuine. An announcement of an impending wedding, birthday, or birth among the hosts results in hundreds of cards, gifts, and flowers from viewers. These faithful viewers call in to talk with the hosts as if they were next-door neighbors or best friends and reveal personal details of their lives. A surprising number of the elderly, the housebound, and the disabled watch the shows.

How does this description of televised shopping relate to children's literature and to the task of evaluating books for whole language? It demonstrates why whole language and children's literature advocates need to exhibit a little less elitism. First, one network, QVC, sells numerous children's books quite below the industry average cost of $17.45 (Roback, 1992). Most of the books are the type that can be purchased in venues other than traditional bookstores. They are the kind of books parents do not mind spending $4 or $5 to purchase. Sometimes they are Golden Books, other times Dr. Seuss collections, and occasionally Disney books. Rarely are the books ones critics and educators recommend or those found on the shelves of children's-only bookstores. The books offered by QVC sell in huge quantities, often selling out. QVC reaches an important segment of the market and informs consumers of the benefits of children's literature in an exciting manner. The hosts convey the impression that they know the latest information about literacy.

Second, the QVC network sells the "Hooked on Phonics" program complete with filmed testimonials from previously illiterate or low-literate individuals. These testimonials detail frustrations with teachers and literacy instruction techniques. All of the individuals in the testimonials state that phonics unlocked the mysteries of reading for them. One host, prior to describing Hooked on Phonics, informed viewers that the problem with "American" education and the reason why Americans could not compete with other industrialized nations was because of the elimination of phonics from the schools. He encouraged viewers to confront teachers, administrators, and school board members and demand explanations for the elimination of phonics. Several viewers called in and agreed with him. Undoubtedly, some individuals took up his challenge. Many more purchased the program.

Third, news organizations, print and electronic, discovered the literacy issue again. CBS's "Sunday Evening News" program of October 4, 1992, featured a segment on whole language, its supporters, and the effects on children. Generally, the segment was favorable, but in the tradition of balanced reporting, the reporter interviewed Professor Jeanne Chall of Harvard, who reiterated her beliefs that phonics instruction in the early grades was essential. In September, the local Champaign-Urbana, Illinois, newspaper printed a letter to the editor that warned of the dire consequences that would result from educators encouraging and teaching "intended spelling" (*invented* spelling is an aspect of the whole-language writing process).

Herein lies a crucial dilemma. Clearly, the public desires information about children's books and whole language, among other literacy topics. Many are making uninformed decisions or using incomplete information acquired from television hosts on shopping networks. The public is less concerned with the process and more concerned with the end product—a child who can read. Publishers of commercial phonics programs have stepped into the void, bypassed educators, and reached the public directly in effective ways through the shopping networks. Supporters of children's literature and whole language are less savvy.

Proponents of whole language need to heed the steps taken by supporters of phonics instruction, whose message has filtered out from universities and professional organizations directly to parents. Whole-language philosophy has not. Parents are confused by concepts such as invented spelling and process writing. Indeed, many teachers are just as confused as parents. They lack a clear understanding of whole language, its underlying principles, and the results that can be achieved from its use.

Having identified the major features of whole language, the criticisms of whole language, and the evaluative criteria helpful in selecting books for whole language, we need now to connect educators and the public with those books.

REFERENCES

Adams, M. J. (1990). *Beginning to read: Thinking and learning about print.* Cambridge, MA: MIT Press.

Au, K. H. (1980). Participation structures in a reading lesson with Hawaiian children: Analysis of culturally appropriate instructional event. *Anthropology and Education Quarterly, 11*(2), 91-115.

Blake, R. (Ed.). (1990). *Whole language: Explorations and applications.* Brockport, NY: New York State English Council.

Chall, J. S. (1983). *Learning to read: The great debate.* New York: McGraw-Hill.

Cullinan, B. E. (1992). Whole language and children's literature. *Language Arts, 69*(6), 426-431.

Delpit, L. D. (1986). Skills and other dilemmas of a progressive Black educator. *Harvard Educational Review, 56*(4), 379-385.

Delpit, L. D. (1988). The silenced dialogue: Power and pedagogy in educating other people's children. *Harvard Educational Review, 58*(3), 280-298.

Dorros, A. (1991). *Abuela.* Illustrated by E. Kleven. New York: Dutton Children's Books.

Goodman, K. S. (1986). *What's whole in whole language?* Portsmouth, NH: Heinemann Educational Books.

Goodman, K. S. (1988). Look what they've done to Judy Blume!: The 'basalization' of children's literature. *New Advocate, 1*(1), 29-41.

Goodman, K. S. (1990). The whole language curriculum. In J. Hydrick & N. Wildermuth (Eds.), *Whole language: Empowerment at the chalk face* (pp. 190-211). New York: Scholastic.

Goodman, K. S. (1992). Why whole language is today's agenda in education. *Language Arts, 69*(5), 354-363.

Goodman, Y. M. (1985). Kidwatching: Observing children in the classroom. In A. Jaggar & M. T. Smith-Burke (Eds.), *Observing the language learner* (pp. 9-18). Newark, DE: International Reading Association.

Groff, P. (1992). Is *RT* a whole language journal? (Letter to the editors). *Reading Teacher, 46*(1), 7.

Hirsch, E. D., Jr. (1987). *Cultural literacy: What every American needs to know.* Boston, MA: Houghton Mifflin.

Hoffman, J. V. (1992). Leadership in the language arts: Am I whole yet? Are you? *Language Arts, 69*(5), 366-371.

Hydrick, J., & Wildermuth, N. (Eds.). (1990) *Whole language: Empowerment at the chalk face.* New York: Scholastic.

Ladson-Billings, G. (1992). Liberatory consequences of literacy: A case of culturally relevant instruction for African American students. *Journal of Negro Education, 61*(3), 378-391.

Langer, J. A.; Applebee, A. N.; Mullis, I. V. S.; & Foertsch, M. A. (1990). *Learning to read in our nation's schools: Instruction and achievement in 1988 at grades 4, 8, and 12.* Princeton, NJ: Educational Testing Service.

Lindgren, M. V. (Ed.). (1991). *The multicolored mirror: Cultural substance in literature for children and young adults.* Fort Atkinson, WI: Highsmith Press.

Lodge, S. (1991, April 26). Growing up too fast? *Publishers Weekly,* pp. 28-32.

Meyer Reimer, K. (1992). Multiethnic literature: Holding fast to dreams. *Language Arts, 69*(1), 14-21.

Roback, D. (1992, January 13). In space, titles, sales, the trend is still up. *Publishers Weekly,* pp. 26-31.

Silvey, A. (1989). The basalization of trade books. *Horn Book Magazine, 65*(5), 549-550.

Sims Bishop, R. (1980). Mirrors, windows, and sliding glass doors. *Perspectives, 6*(3), ix-xi.

Teale, W. H. (1992). A talk with Carole Edelsky about politics and literacy. *Language Arts, 69*(5), 324-329.

Wong Fillmore, L., & Valadez, C. (1986). Teaching bilingual learners. In M. C. Wittrock (Ed.), *Handbook of research on teaching* (3rd ed., pp. 648-685). New York: Macmillan.

BETTY CARTER

Associate Professor
School of Library and Information Studies
Texas Woman's University
Denton, Texas

Reviewing Nonfiction Books for Children and Young Adults: Stance, Scholarship, and Structure

INTRODUCTION

Both the writing and the reviewing of children's and young adult nonfiction are art forms. Fine works of nonfiction promise hours of pleasure, exhilaration, and contemplation for their readers; they convey both wonder and passion about a particular topic or theme; and, to paraphrase Robert Probst (1986), they feed a child's thinking rather than control it. At best, nonfiction books are characterized by beautifully written prose, definable themes, unifying structure, and stimulating subjects.

Likewise, so are fine reviews. They don't simply indicate a thumbs up/thumbs down recommendation, but instead impart a sense of the book as a whole, discuss what subject is covered as well as how it is presented, and suggest ways to extend a book and thus bring it to more readers. Reviews not only introduce specific titles to librarians, teachers, parents, and booksellers, who in turn share them with young people, but they also feed the profession's thinking about matters concerning the nature of literature.

Not surprisingly, the best reviewers are readers—readers who devour books rather than simply pick them up to satisfy the demands of their jobs; readers who surround themselves with books, and words, and ideas; and readers who want to share these passions with others. Frequently, though, their literary love affairs begin with the traditional triumvirate of fiction, poetry, and drama, and it is that particular genre orientation that unconsciously affects the ways in which they interact with all subsequent books they encounter.

THE STATUS OF NONFICTION

Story is powerful. It has pulled many individuals into children's and young adult literature, and it remains an influential force in both professional and personal lives. From parable to allegory, fairy tale to novel, poem to play, and myth to narrative, story can challenge readers to face potent truths and perpetual themes that reflect the very essence of the human condition. With such a strong heritage, it's no wonder that these formats dominate both the professional literature and the review media.

Yet other equally respectable, if not respected, patterns appear in children's and young adult literature. That Brent Ashabranner (1989) chooses topical outline to honor the Vietnam War Memorial, or that Brenda Guiberson (1992) uses compare/contrast to introduce readers to *Spoonbill Swamp*, or that Hanna Machotka (1992) employs a series of questions and answers to arouse curiosity in the readers of *Breathtaking Noses*, must be recognized as different, rather than inferior, ways of organizing text material. Books featuring such non-narrative patterns as cause/effect, topical outline, and question/answer deserve respect. What the profession needs to ask itself is, "Do such books get the same consideration as do narrative accounts?"

To examine this question, I recently tallied the starred reviews, or those books of special distinction recommended for children and young adults, that appeared in *Booklist, The Bulletin of the Center for Children's Books, The Horn Book Magazine,* and *School Library Journal* from January 1991 through June 1992. During that period, 461 separate titles were starred; 110 of these books received stars from more than one journal. Of these starred reviews, 274, or 59.4%, were fiction titles, while 187, or 40.5%, were nonfiction.

Although the above distribution appears fairly even, notice what happens when 105 (of the 187) starred reviews for poetry, folklore, and biography are eliminated from the count. That leaves 82, or 17.7% of the total starred reviews, that can be defined as informational books. Of those 82, almost 20% are narrative nonfiction (having some form of story in it): books such as Ina Chang's (1991) *A Separate Battle: Women and the Civil War,* or Jill Krementz's (1992) *How It Feels to Live with a Physical Disability,* or Iris Van Rynbach's (1991) *Everything from a Nail to a Coffin,* or Owen Beattie and John Geiger's (1992) *Buried in Ice: The Mystery of a Lost Arctic Expedition* contain strong narrative threads.

Fifteen years ago, Milton Meltzer, quoting Aidan Chambers on the status of nonfiction, wrote: "While it has not been completely ignored . . . nonfiction 'does get brushed off and pushed to the back . . . as though information books were socially inferior to the upper-crust stuff we call literature. . . . We'd do better by children, and ourselves if we revised its accepted definition to include all that is published. . . . Every book, no matter what its content and purpose, deserves and demands the respect and treatment—the skill and care—of art'" (Meltzer, 1976, p. 19). The figures from the above exercise suggest that nonfiction may still get "pushed to the back," and that perhaps stories, narratives, biographies, poetry, and folklore enjoy the most favored genre status in our review journals. To negate this charge, responsible reviewers must ask themselves if they are, first of all, unconsciously responding positively to story narrative because they prefer that format, and, second, if they are slighting nonfiction because it does not mirror their personal reading preferences.

REVIEWING INFORMATIONAL BOOKS

Keep in mind, though, that no reviewer should praise mediocre titles just to even out these numbers. Some of the nonfiction that is published should understandably be "pushed to the back" of the literary shelf. Here one should find those books that merely assemble data on topics such as the states, inventions, or the solar system. Unfortunately, the weakest of these have precipitated the strongest professional bias against nonfiction: Informational books primarily exist to satisfy demands for assigned reports.

To make matters worse, these publications become a part of a self-fulfilling prophecy: More books are written to meet these requirements; research is designed to respond to available materials; and children, forced to engage in such meaningless activities, ultimately become the losers. Make no mistake, this circle is not the creation of reviewers; it is constructed by both educators and publishers. Reviewers, however, must refrain from feeding this publishing frenzy and must discontinue the practice of recommending books by discussing subject and simply adding the lone positive statement that they are "useful for school reports."

Why is the inclusion of this tag line so offensive? The combined weight of the sheer numbers of such books, and the frequency with which these volumes are recommended for school reports, not only reinforce the utilitarian stereotype, but also may well stand in the way of librarians and teachers purchasing and recommending outstanding books that deviate from this assumed norm.

In addition, the assumption that a book will be "useful for school reports" typically rests on the premise that assignments consist of teacher-directed research that seeks solutions to finite, specific, and answerable questions. Certainly many projects do, but not all. School districts across the country are opening up student inquiry through I-searches (personal research), interdisciplinary projects, and community activities. Would the book typically recommended as "useful for school reports" help or hinder these students? In addition, does the repetition of such a comment eventually validate unimaginative projects that demand little more from the student than the ability to list the imports and exports of a particular country?

If not pejorative, "useful for school reports" certainly delivers faint praise. Of the 82 starred reviews of informational books, only 3 mentioned school assignments. In each case, "the school assignment" recommendation was tempered by noting the potential for recreational reading and browsing, or by suggesting that a resulting report would be both unusual and different. Such comments set up a double standard between fiction and nonfiction. Since less than successful novels are not recommended as appropriate titles for book reports, weak nonfiction books should not be suggested as fitting vehicles for research. Instead, reviewers will better serve their audience if they come clean about a book's strengths and weaknesses. If a book has a clear organizational structure, then comment on that; if the topics covered are logical components of the whole, then mention that feature; and if the index is accessible, then point it out. On the other hand, if a writer's style is uninspired and dry, alert both the review audience and the author, instead of excusing this limitation by sending the book to the research shelf. By concentrating on the features of a particular book, reviewers won't encourage the groundless assumption that nonfiction only satisfies school demands.

Reviewers can additionally dispel the book-correlates-with-report notion by suggesting alternative ways to introduce and extend those nonfiction volumes that treat topics and themes with both style and substance. In a recent interview for the *ALAN Review*, Sally Estes, editor of books for youth at *Booklist*, mentions that "They're [review journals] intended to keep readers up to date with what's new, what's good, and perhaps to suggest ways these books can be used with the target audience" (Carter, 1992, p. 52).

Hazel Rochman, assistant editor of books for youth at *Booklist*, suggests ways these books can be used with the target audience by recommending nonfiction for reading aloud, a practice not widely considered by many in the literary community (Carter & Abrahamson, 1991). In another departure from the norm, Rochman's (1991a, 1991b) recommended read-alouds frequently include non-narrative volumes such as *Antler, Bear, Canoe: A Northwoods Alphabet Year* (Bowen, 1991) or *A Sea Full of Sharks* (Maestro & Maestro, 1990). Similarly, Carolyn Phelan's (1992) review of *Wonderful Pussy Willows* (Wexler, 1992) lets teachers and librarians know that the book can be expanded by following the clear directions for growing pussy willows from seed or by grafting, while Ellen Fader's (1992) review of *Dinosaurs to the Rescue!: A Guide to Protecting Our Planet* (Brown & Brown, 1992) mentions that children can participate in improving the environment through projects, such as making milk carton bird feeders, which should easily find natural outlets in both classrooms and libraries.

CHILDREN AND NONFICTION

These suggestions, along with comments such as Kathryn Pierson Jennings' recommendation that *On the Air* (Hautzig, 1991) would be a likely candidate "for young non-fiction readers who 'just want a good book'" (Jennings, 1992, p. 181), underscore the premise that children do indeed find pleasure in nonfiction. Sometimes that pleasure comes from finding themselves within the pages of particular volumes, and sometimes that pleasure comes from the facts and information they take away from the books.

Readers can interact with books in one of two ways. They can either look for what they can experience through text, or they can concentrate on what they can take away from text. Lifetime readers, or those adults who regularly read books for both information and pleasure, write of the emotional involvement they experienced with books when they were children and young adults (Carlsen & Sherrill, 1988). Aliterate youth, on the other hand, express no connection with books at all. One junior high student summed up these feelings: "You open the book. You look at the words. You close the book. Big deal" (Beers, 1990, p. 136).

Consequently, librarians, teachers, and parents who wish to help children become lifetime readers try to recommend books that will trigger emotional responses. Many adults, coming from reading backgrounds dominated by fiction, assume that nonfiction, with its information and facts, provides the forum for taking information away from text, while fiction, with its characters and story line, supplies the vehicle for encountering experiences through text. This assumption defines the reader as a passive individual who simply follows the dictates of an author and implies that text ultimately determines a reader's stance.

In practice, readers define their own individual stances, and, like literary switch-hitters, frequently shift from one to another within a single text.

These are the children who open Robert C. O'Brien's (1971) *Mrs. Frisby and the Rats of NIMH* and discover that NIMH is not a product of the author's imagination but the National Institute of Mental Health. Such readers take this and other specific information away from the novel. By the final chapter, however, these very readers often identify with both characters and story and find themselves vicariously involved in the action. They wonder if they would be brave enough to defend a noble idea as the rats did. Would they trade their creature comforts for a harsher, yet more honorable, life?

On the other side of the coin are those nonfiction readers of Seymour Simon's (1989) *Whales* who may learn that the heart of a blue whale is the size of a small car or that some whales dive to depths as great as a mile. Again, these youngsters will quickly alter their stances and engage in personal responses by wondering what it would be like if they were to see or photograph or swim with a whale. Neither author nor literary form has dictated these responses; the individual readers have.

Other readers choose not to find their identification, and thus their pleasure and information, vicariously. These children seek active participation from books. They are the youngsters who may tune out Russell Freedman's (1987) well-crafted descriptions of Lincoln's tortured soul in *Lincoln: A Photobiography*, but see the physical results of our 16th president's blackest hours in the deep facial lines they try to re-create when using Lee J. Ames' (1978) *Draw 50 Famous Faces* to sketch his portrait. Their personal stances will come through literature, not by identifying with a character, but rather by engaging in text and actively creating meaning as they physically respond to this popular informational book. Adults must recognize and support such individual literary choices.

Consider a recent ethnographic study conducted by Kylene Beers (1990) that examined aliterate junior high students. Beers spent months in the classroom observing and talking to those young adults who are able to read but chose not to. What she found was that even these uncommitted and unmotivated students did read something; they read nonfiction. But, said one aliterate student, "I don't think the teacher would call what I'm doing reading" (Beers, 1990, p. 167).

Unfortunately, what many youngsters have learned is that according to many adults, fiction is reading; nonfiction is not. By publicly recognizing that nonfiction readers will find pleasure and create meaning with the books they choose, reviewers can help break this stereotype.

DOCUMENTATION IN NONFICTION

Without a doubt, reviewers can effect change in the profession. In 1986 Hazel Rochman questioned authors and publishers who did not include documentation in their nonfiction offerings. Prior to this discussion, few nonfiction books contained complete documentation, or author's notes, acknowledgments, text referencing, footnotes, and/ or bibliographies (Rochman, 1986).

Yet, three years later, when Dick Abrahamson and I interviewed seven authors for our book *Nonfiction for Young Adults: From Delight to Wisdom* (Carter & Abrahamson, 1990), we discovered that each clearly wrestled with this issue, and the impetus to do so came from reviewers. As Brent Ashabranner told us:

> I have benefited from reviews. I am happy to say that most of the reviews of my books have been favorable, but occasionally a reviewer points out something that helps me in future books. For example, I learned early on that reviewers of books for teenage readers take documentation of what the writer says very seriously. I wasn't paying sufficient attention to documentation, and after the first book or two that I wrote, I've been much more careful about letting my readers know where I got my information. I put it into the text in a way that doesn't interfere with the prose but assures the reader that I didn't just make things up. I've been much more careful with my bibliographies. Thoughtful reviews help me be a better writer. (Carter & Abrahamson, 1990, p. 101)

In a similar interview, Milton Meltzer shares the reasons for his resistance to source notes:

> I think bibliographies are very important. Recently I have been including annotated bibliographies, organized by subjects covered in the text. This helps give the young reader an indication of the nature of the book, what it's about, and ought to be more valuable than just the listing of titles. I also indicate which reference books may be the most useful to them. Now, on the issue of footnotes, there is a difference of opinion. Hazel Rochman, at *Booklist*, thinks that the text itself should have footnotes, either at the back of the book or at the bottom of each page. I suspect a great many young readers would be put off by all these notes. I try to refer, within the text, to the source of important statements or facts and to indicate whether something is disputed. But I don't provide scholarly footnotes for young readers. All sources—books, magazines, newspapers, journals—will be in the bibliography. If I were to put footnotes into my books there might be as many as ten or fifteen on every single page. (Carter & Abrahamson, 1990, p. 54)

This interview doesn't contain Meltzer's last word on the subject. His most recent release, *The Amazing Potato*, includes an informal, yet informative, discussion of sources in chapter by chapter notes appended to the text. Neither dry nor pedantic, these source notes underscore Meltzer's scholarship and acknowledge that some of his readers may well want to explore related subjects on their own (Meltzer, 1992).

Nonfiction will frequently act as the agent that brings a child and a particular subject or field of study together. That's how James Jensen, or Dinosaur Jim, was introduced to his life-long dream. Jensen writes: "My father bought a used geology textbook, and in the back of it were pictures of dinosaurs. While some boys dreamed of a new bicycle, I dreamed of finding dinosaurs. I would always wake up before I could dig them up. I never did have a bicycle, but I've never stopped dreaming of dinosaurs" (Wilford, 1985, p. 8).

Similarly, Richard Wright discovered his life's work through nonfiction. In his case, it was the essays of H. L. Mencken. In *Black Boy* he comments: "Yes, this man was fighting, fighting with words. He was using words as a weapon, using them as one would use a club. Could words be weapons? Well, yes, for here they were. Then, maybe, perhaps, I could use them as a weapon?" (Wright, 1945, p. 272).

And Pulitzer Prize winner Annie Dillard writes of being a teenager and being given a book on plants. She read the words, thought about the images, and performed some of the simple experiments. Dillard concludes her memory with these powerful words: "I had a life" (Dillard, 1987, p. 149).

As Hazel Rochman points out, shoddy or nonexistent documentation delivers a disturbing message from authors to readers: "Trust me. I've looked at the evidence, and I'll tell you" (Rochman, 1986, p. 639). This attitude reflects the antithesis of critical reading skills—never to accept unquestioningly what is in print, always to check statistics and sources, and to think independently—that form the core of respected school curricula. Professional educators cannot develop critical thinkers or budding scientists, writers, and historians if the raw materials they use encourage passivity.

In addition, the inclusion of specific attribution lets readers know that research happens before writing begins. Youngsters who are asked to write assume that adult authors are either born knowing the information they share in books or that they acquire that information through exotic life experiences. The perpetual advice, "Write about something you know," is repeated in classrooms across the country. But this recommendation proves futile unless children and young adults encounter models for acquiring that information. If these readers never see examples of an author's research, then the inevitable conclusion—that they can't begin to write because they just don't possess enough information—appears perfectly logical.

Even the youngest of writers will find models for their personal publications in the books they read. First-grade authors regularly include title pages, tables of contents, and chapters in their own books since they view these elements as integral parts of a reputable whole. Likewise, these youngsters will also put acknowledgments, an author's note, and even bibliographical information in their own writing if they've also encountered these features. Authors do more than impart information to children. The books youngsters read become literary role models for their own writing and inquiry.

Still, the argument persists that footnotes and bibliographies are off-putting to children, and that young readers will not pick up books that include such features. The problem here is that we simply don't know whether or not this assumption is valid. It may be another one of those self-fulfilling prophecies that sustain themselves in the nonfiction world: Books are published without documentation, children read those books, so more books are published without evidence of scholarship. Until researchers examine this notion, publishers should err on the side of accuracy by including acknowledgments, bibliographies, and specific citations. If such documentation is appended, then readers may choose to explore or ignore it.

Fine nonfiction, as Aidan Chambers said, deserves "the respect and treatment—the skill and care—of art" (Meltzer, 1976, p. 19). The diverse writings of Sir Francis Bacon, John Locke, Abraham Lincoln, Loren Eisley, Jane Addams, Joseph Brunner, Stephen Hawking, and Barbara Tuchman have not only recorded the human experience, but they've also defined it. From Thomas Paine's *Common Sense* to Albert Einstein's $E = mc^2$ to Carl Sagan's *Cosmos* to Martin Luther King Jr.'s *Letter from a Birmingham Jail* to John F. Kennedy's *Profiles in Courage* to Betty Friedan's *Feminine Mystique* to John L. Soule's plea to go west, nonfiction—with its stirring language, its compelling subjects, and its impressive abilities to provoke thought and challenge beliefs—has shaped philosophies, societies, and individuals.

STYLE AND STRUCTURE

While juvenile nonfiction doesn't have the global impact of its adult counterpart, it does frequently challenge and inspire many of its young readers. Sometimes this stimulation comes through an interesting subject. Often it doesn't. The genius of Jim Giblin (1987), for example, is that he can turn a discussion of knives, forks, and spoons into a social commentary that challenges readers to think about previously unrelated topics from technology, history, and culture. Giblin's control over both style and structure makes this possible.

Good reviewers discuss style. They note the clarity with which Russell Freedman (1991) discusses lift in *The Wright Brothers*, they point out Seymour Simon's (1990) ability to explain the tidal pull in *Oceans*, and they frequently excerpt portions of text to back up their opinions. Less frequently though, do reviewers comment on structure.

Specific facts and opinions represent what the author wants to offer the reader; structure determines how the author wants the reader to think about that subject. Brent Ashabranner admits that finding an appropriate "structure may take him almost as long to locate as the actual writing takes" (Ashabranner, 1988, p. 751). Similarly, Jean Fritz reiterates the importance of structure when she writes: "The art of fiction is making up facts; the art of nonfiction is using facts to make up a form" (Fritz, 1988, p. 759).

Unlike style, which meshes with subject, structure controls subject. Readers of Lisa Westberg Peters' *The Sun, the Wind and the Rain*, for example, consider the evolution of a mountain not as a historical process, but as an event that parallels a young girl building a sand mountain at the beach. Peters (1990) sets up the compare/contrast structure with the opening sentence: "This is the story of two mountains. The earth made one. Elizabeth in her yellow sun hat made the other" (p. 1).

Mature readers look for such organizational patterns and structure their reading and their thinking around them. When reading a chronological history, for example, they key in on those reported events that happened first, then second, and then third. They are thus able to eliminate asides and appositives that have little relationship to the whole while retaining more crucial information within a familiar perceptual frame. When reading John Langone's (1992) *Our Endangered Earth*, for instance, readers will expect to encounter a solution after reading about a problem, and another problem after reading the previous solution. And those readers of Ken Robbins' (1990) *A Flower Grows* expect to continue with his sequential progression until the end of the book. Consequently, these readers begin to anticipate what will happen next rather than look for a tangential discussion of parallel events.

Patterns such as enumeration, sequence, cause/effect, and compare/contrast not only control subject in a book, but they also provide youngsters with models for organizing information. This is the language of grown-ups. The profession's infatuation with narrative, even narrative in nonfiction, may result in many outstanding works, but it may not be an unmitigated good. As Linda Levistik comments, "History is more than narrative. It is also learning to sift evidence before it has been shaped and interpreted" (Levistik, 1992, p. 13). To help children sift through evidence, librarians and teachers need to provide books on a variety of topics presented with a variety of structures. They will discover these books through the review media.

Enumeration, or topical outline, represents the most frequently used organizational pattern for information books. In such works, writers describe their subjects by examining what they believe to be the relevant parts of that whole. The second most common pattern found in informational books is that of time or chronological order. Since these two patterns appear so frequently, they are less likely to be mentioned in reviews. Still, conscientious reviewers such as Roger Sutton, executive editor for *The Bulletin of the Center for Children's Books,* manage to work them in. Notice how he clues his readers into the chronological sequence of Doris Epler's (1992) *The Berlin Wall:* "Epler's tidy history of the Wall ends with German reunification; it begins with the economic and political disruption of the Weimar Republic that led to Nazism, World War II, and the subsequent determination by the Allies that Germany would never again be a threat. Clearly outlining the postwar tensions which led to the building of the Wall, as well as those exacerbated by the Wall itself, Epler provides a comprehensive context for the Wall's destruction" (Sutton, 1992a, p. 178).

Frequently authors will use several patterns within a book. A chronological narrative describes John Kennedy's early years in Barbara Harrison and Daniel Terris' (1992) biography, *A Twilight Struggle: The Life of John Fitzgerald Kennedy.* Yet, when they deal with Kennedy's presidency, the authors deftly move from this pattern to expository chapters on topics such as domestic policies, foreign affairs, and the arts. Again, reviewers should notify readers of these shifts. Gail Gibbons (1992), in *The Great St. Lawrence Seaway* for example, uses both chronological sequence and enumeration, a dual pattern obvious to readers of this review: "Gibbons' account of the Seaway begins in 1535 with the French explorations; she goes on to show the early canals, settlements, and the first lock, built in 1779. The four-panel demonstration of how this lock works is a good introduction to the more intricate (if essentially the same) operations of the system today, shown through the experiences of one large 'laker' as it progresses from the Atlantic, through the fifteen locks of the Seaway, to Gary, Indiana" (Sutton, 1992b, p. 179).

CONCLUSION

With over 5,000 children's and young adult books published every year, librarians, teachers, parents, and booksellers must rely on review journals for opinions about titles, authors, and trends. Since review sources have such an impact on the field, their treatment of both specific titles and books in general influences the reception of those works. The best reviewers don't take these responsibilities lightly; they respect both books and readers. They don't operate from a preset checklist and tally up an appropriate number of points to determine a book's final rating. Instead, they evaluate each book as a whole, giving it "the respect and treatment—the skill and care—of art" (Meltzer, 1976, p. 19).

REFERENCES

Ames, L. J. (1978). *Draw 50 famous faces*. New York: Doubleday.

Ashabranner, B. (1988). Did you really write that for children? *Horn Book Magazine, 64*(6), 749-754.

Ashabranner, B. (1989). *Always to remember: The story of the Vietnam Veterans Memorial*. New York: Putnam.

Beattie, O., & Geiger, J. (1992). *Buried in ice: The mystery of a lost arctic expedition*. New York: Scholastic.

Beers, G. K. (1990). *Choosing not to read: An ethnographic study of seventh-grade aliterate students*. Unpublished doctoral dissertation, University of Houston.

Bowen, B. (1991). *Antler, bear, canoe: A northwoods alphabet year*. Boston, MA: Joy Street Books.

Brown, L. K., & Brown, M. T. (1992). *Dinosaurs to the rescue!: A guide to protecting our planet*. Boston, MA: Little, Brown.

Carlsen, R. G., & Sherrill, A. (1988). *Voices of readers: How we come to love books*. Urbana, IL: National Council of Teachers of English.

Carter, B. (1992). So many books, so little time: An interview with Sally Estes, editor at *Booklist*. *ALAN Review, 20*(1), 52-55.

Carter, B., & Abrahamson, R. F. (1990). *Nonfiction for young adults: From delight to wisdom*. Phoenix, AZ: Oryx Press.

Carter, B., & Abrahamson, R. F. (1991). Nonfiction in a read-aloud program. *Journal of Reading, 34*(8), 638-642.

Chang, I. (1991). *A separate battle: Women and the Civil War*. New York: Lodestar Books.

Cummings, P. (Comp. & Ed.). (1992). *Talking with artists*. New York: Bradbury.

Dillard, A. (1987). *An American childhood*. New York: Harper & Row.

Epler, D. M. (1992). *The Berlin Wall: How it rose and why it fell*. Brookfield, CT: Millbrook Press.

Fader, E. (1992). Review of *Dinosaurs to the rescue!: A guide to protecting our planet* by L. K. Brown and M. Brown. *Horn Book Magazine, 68*(4), 464-465.

Freedman, R. (1987). *Lincoln: A photobiography*. New York: Clarion Books.

Freedman, R. (1991). *The Wright brothers: How they invented the airplane*. New York: Holiday House.

Fritz, J. (1988). Biography: Readability plus responsibility. *Horn Book Magazine, 64*(6), 759-760.

Gibbons, G. (1992). *The great St. Lawrence Seaway*. New York: Morrow Junior Books.

Giblin, J. C. (1987). *From hand to mouth, or, How we invented knives, forks, spoons, and chopsticks & the table manners to go with them*. New York: Crowell.

Guiberson, B. Z. (1992). *Spoonbill swamp*. Illustrated by M. Lloyd. New York: Holt.

Harrison, B., & Terris, D. (1992). *The twilight struggle: The life of John Fitzgerald Kennedy*. New York: Lothrop, Lee & Shepard.

Hautzig, E. K. (1991). *On the air: Behind the scenes at a TV newscast*. Illustrated by D. R. Hautzig. New York: Macmillan.

Jennings, K. P. (1992). Review of *On the air: Behind the scenes at a TV newscast* by E. Hautzig. *Bulletin of the Center for Children's Books, 45*(7), 180-181.

Krementz, J. (1992). *How it feels to live with a physical disability*. New York: Simon & Schuster.

Langone, J. (1992). *Our endangered earth: Our fragile environment and what we can do to save it*. Boston, MA: Little, Brown.

Levistik, L. (1992). *Mediating content through literary texts: Mediating literary texts in elementary classrooms.* Paper presented at the Annual Meeting of the American Educational Research Association, San Francisco, CA.

Machotka, H. (1992). *Breathtaking noses.* New York: Morrow Junior Books.

Maestro, B., & Maestro, G. (1990). *A sea full of sharks.* New York: Scholastic.

Meltzer, M. (1976). Where do all the prizes go? The case for nonfiction. *Horn Book Magazine, 52*(1), 17-23.

Meltzer, M. (1992). *The amazing potato: A story in which the Incas, Conquistadors, Marie Antoinette, Thomas Jefferson, wars, famines, immigrants, and French fries all play a part.* New York: HarperCollins.

O'Brien, R. C. (1971). *Mrs. Frisby and the rats of NIMH.* Illustrated by Z. Bernstein. New York: Atheneum.

Peters, L. W. (1990). *The sun, the wind and the rain.* New York: Holt.

Phelan, C. (1992). Review of *Wonderful pussy willows* by J. Wexler. *Booklist, 88*(17), 1599.

Probst, R. E. (1986). Three relationships in the teaching of literature. *English Journal, 75*(1), 60-68.

Robbins, Ken. (1990). *A flower grows.* New York: Dial.

Rochman, H. (1986). The YA connection: Footnotes and critical thinking. *Booklist, 83*(8), 639.

Rochman, H. (1991a). Review of *A sea full of sharks* by B. Maestro and G. Maestro. *Booklist, 87*(10), 1058.

Rochman, H. (1991b). Review of *Antler, bear, canoe: A northwoods alphabet year* by B. Bowen. *Booklist, 88*(5), 526.

Simon, S. (1989). *Whales.* New York: Crowell.

Simon, S. (1990). *Oceans.* New York: Morrow Junior Books.

Sutton, R. (1992a). Review of *The Berlin Wall: How it rose and why it fell* by D. M. Epler. *Bulletin of the Center for Children's Books, 45*(7), 178-179.

Sutton, R. (1992b). Review of *The great St. Lawrence Seaway* by G. Gibbons. *Bulletin of the Center for Children's Books, 45*(7), 179.

Van Rynbach, I. (1991). *Everything from a nail to a coffin.* New York: Orchard Books.

Wexler, J. (1992). *Wonderful pussy willows.* New York: Dutton Children's Books.

Wilford, J. N. (1985). *The riddle of the dinosaur.* New York: Knopf.

Wright, R. (1945). *Black boy: A record of childhood and youth.* New York: Harper & Row.

BARBARA KIEFER

Associate Professor
Teachers College Columbia University
New York, New York

Visual Criticism and Children's Literature

INTRODUCTION

Imagine an audience sitting enthralled as a storyteller unfolds a picture book tale. Pictures add form and feeling, color and depth as the words pour forth. The participants in this event have different responses. Some do not move their eyes from the pictures for a moment. Others look first to the pictures, then back to the face of the narrator in a continual, rhythmic movement. Still others, further back in the group, take in the entire event, teller, image, and audience, but they see the smallest detail and remember it. For all present, the event takes on a magical quality. Each participant is called upon to engage in interchange of intellect and emotion, an experience that is at once communal as well as individual and that transcends time and place. Indeed, the scene is timeless. It could take place in front of the cave paintings at Lascaux 15,000 years ago or in the Warlpiri culture in the western Australian desert today.

Those in the field of library science or education are more likely to recognize it as a scene from the library or classroom story time. But the importance of this type of visual/verbal experience is no less powerful because it is mainly experienced by children in Western culture. Suzanne Langer (1942) has argued that, "Image-making is . . . the mode of our untutored thinking, and stories are its earliest products" (p. 145). The long tradition of the picture book, then, grows out of some essential human characteristic that over the centuries has been the result of a cultural need to represent some basic aspect of the individual and the race through image and myth, and an artist's need to convey some

73

meaning through visual symbols (Kiefer, 1989). In ensuing years, the changing needs of society, as reflected in the culture of a given age, have determined the content of the picture book and designated the audience, while technological advances have allowed the medium of the experience to expand beyond the wall of a cave or the floor of the desert to laser reproductions of all manner of original works, bound in paper between the covers of a book.

Moreover, just as the cave paintings of Lascaux, the illuminated manuscripts of the Middle Ages, and the "dreamings" of Australian aborigines are usually the province of art historians, today's picture books are art objects and must be subject to a similar visual criticism. For a picture book relies as much or more on visual meaning as it does on verbal meaning.

CRITICISM AND PICTURE BOOKS

Marantz (1977), for example, has argued that picture books are not literature, that is, word-dominated creations, but rather a form of visual art that must be experienced as a visual/verbal entity. Bader (1976) suggests that the picture book is an art form that "hinges on the interdependence of pictures and words, on the simultaneous display of two facing pages, and on the drama of the turning of the page" (p. 1). The fact that with picture books we are dealing at the very least with two different codes or systems of communication complicates a task that even within the realms of purely visual or purely verbal criticism is always a difficult one. Often critics attempt to relate the picture book to conventions of criticism in one or the other discipline instead of dealing with the art of the picture book as a separate and unique entity. For years, reviewers of picture books have been taken to task for neglecting the pictures or relegating discussion of art elements to a few stock phrases or words. More recently, theories of visual literacy have been developed, but too often these liken the art to verbal elements or treat reading pictures as akin to reading words or reading signs. On the other hand, some scholars have categorized the illustrations in books according to traditional categories of art history, for example, impressionistic, expressionistic, realistic, or abstract and have thus suggested that styles of illustrations are synonymous with styles of painting.

Useful theories regarding the art of the picture book have, I believe, developed out of the field of semiotic theory. In this context, scholars have developed theories of various relationships of pictures and text. Golden (1990), for example, proposes five different relationships between illustrations and text in picture books. In three of these relationships, she argues, the illustrations play a complementary, extending, or highlighting role, but the text can be read separate from the pictures without any essential loss of meaning. In the other two relationships that she suggests, the illustrations either provide information crucial to the written text or clarify and go beyond information in the words. Here the pictures must be present if all information is to be obtained.

Nodelman (1988) has suggested that the relationship between pictures and text is always an ironic one, that is, "the words tell us what the pictures do not show, and the pictures show us what the words do not tell" (p. 222). He argues, for example that

> when words and pictures combine, irony emerges from the way in which the incompleteness of each is revealed by the differing incompleteness of the other. The theoretically "fierce bad rabbit" in Beatrix Potter's book of that name looks soft and cuddly, anything but the evil creature that the text refers to. (p. 223)

While an understanding of verbal/pictorial relationships might help us to "deconstruct" a particular picture book, however, it does not necessarily move us to a theory of criticism. The pictures in *Titch* (Hutchins, 1971), which according to Golden function almost as a caption, are no less effective than the pictures in *Dr. DeSoto* (Steig, 1982), which are necessary to an understanding of the written text. I would argue, with Langer, that the fabric of *meaning* is at the essence of any art form. Thus, in setting forth a theory of visual criticism in picture books, it seems important to understand how it is that the art conveys meaning rather than just to categorize the pictures according to periods of art history or to identify their relationship to text.

THE AESTHETIC NATURE OF THE PICTURE BOOK

In considering any mode of communication, visual, verbal, or an interaction between the two, it is important to understand how meaning is expressed and understood within that form. While both language and visual art have a meaning-expressing potential, the two are not identical and cannot be matched at a "word" or "sentence" level. Furthermore, the result of engagements with visual and verbal texts may be very different. Nodelman (1988) suggests, for example, "that the visual spaces depicted in pictures imply time and that the temporal sequences depicted in words imply space" (p. 243). Gombrich (1982) argues that while both language and visual images have the capacity to express, arouse, and describe, the visual image is most effective in evoking emotions while it is unable to match "the statement function of language" (p. 138).

On the other hand, when considering how meaning is expressed, verbal and visual art have much in common. Both the author and the artist have elements available for conveying meaning. The author uses sounds and words, the phonetic and morphemic systems of language. The artist uses line, shape, color, value, and texture, the elements of art. Both language and art have syntactic and semantic properties. Hellman (1977), for example, argues that we recognize the syntactic properties of art, such as the organization of lines and color, but also the semantic properties in which lines and colors evoke moods such as quiet, warm, or angry. In addition, authors and artists have in common principles of organization which both refer to as composition. Moreover, aspects of composition such as balance, rhythm, and pattern are common to both. Finally, the word *style* is applied to the product created as a result of authors' or artists' choices of these elements and principles. The fact that the concept of style is applied to both literature and art and that it is linked with the expression of meaning makes style a proper basis for a theory of visual criticism in picture books.

STYLE IN ART

Style as the term is used in art has been the subject of considerable debate, just as it has been in literary fields. The term *style* has been used to describe the work of individuals as well as that of cultures and eras. Novitz (1976) attempted to clarify the term by differentiating between pictorial styles, artistic styles, and personal styles. Pictorial styles, he explains, are distinguished by certain "widely accepted procedures of depicting . . . called 'umbrella' conventions" (p. 336). Falling in this category would be the use of perspective or impressionistic perceptions. That is, artists of the early Renaissance began using newly discovered formulas of perspective, while impressionist painters were those who were interested in the immediate image captured by the eye before the brain had time to clarify or define it. On the other hand, artistic styles might involve changes in emphasis or in subject matter but not in overall methods of depicting—the Renaissance style as opposed to mannerism or the movement from religious or classical subject matter of the Renaissance to the homey interiors of Dutch genre painting. Finally, individuals might work in the same pictorial and artistic styles, but idiosyncratic features would help distinguish one artist's picture from another—Michelangelo from Raphael or Monet from Pissarro.

A point of consensus in discussions of style in art seems to be the dual quality of style. Wolfflin (1932) referred to "the double root of style"; Hellman (1977) discusses *exemplified* and *expressed* properties (syntactic and semantic). Thus, any consideration of style must consider not only the formal objective properties of style but those subjective properties that lead to an expression of meaning.

Genova (1979) proposed a "meaning-expressing model" for style, acknowledging "a variety of sources ranging from psychological to cultural and aesthetic ones," but emphasizing that style was the result of unconscious as well as conscious choices (p. 324). Her crucial point, however, was that style is symbolic of meaning. The two are "inextricably interwoven; they reflect, express and constitute each other," she argued (p. 323).

Following these understandings, then, style might be defined most simply as "manner of expressing." The meaning of the word "express," to make known, reveal, show, is in keeping with the dual nature of style. The word "manner" can be understood to encompass all the conscious as well as unconscious choices the artist embraces in order to "make known." Aspects of style such as formal elements, techniques, and pictorial conventions, then, represent a field of choices available to the artist in order to accomplish the primary purpose of expressing meaning.

STYLE IN PICTURE BOOKS

Although I have been discussing a theory of style that grows out of the field of visual art, these understandings—with some modifications and additions—may be applied to the art of picture books. Both the painter and the illustrator choose elements of art, principles of composition, and historical and cultural conventions that may be highly effective in expressing meaning. However, in executing a painting, an artist may choose to envision a story, capture a moment in history or time, explore an intellectual vision, or express some purely inner feeling with little care or concern for how an audience will perceive the finished product. The illustrator, on the other hand, is bound to a specific idea or narrative, with some intent, at least, to convey a specific meaning to an audience. Moreover, while the painter is concerned with a single image on one pictorial plane, the illustrator is bound to a sequence of images, sometimes in the company of written text, sometimes not. Finally, while the painter is faced with choices of media, for example, oil or acrylic, the illustrator must consider, in addition, not only original media but also other technical choices inherent in the reproduction of the work within the covers of a book. These technical choices may also be expressive of meaning and add to or detract from the overall aesthetic experience possible with a given book.

Marantz (1977) has argued that "art objects are important because they have the potential for producing a transcendental experience, a state of mind where new and personal meanings can take shape" (p. 151). This, I believe, is the essence of the aesthetic experience possible as a result of a good picture book. In the remainder of this paper, I will explore several categories of stylistic choices that grow out of the above understandings, attempting to show how they apply to the art of illustration and add to or affect the quality of the picture book and the overall aesthetic experience.

In judging the quality of a picture book, the critic must begin with the verbal text, or in the case of a concept book or wordless picture book, with the idea or theme of the book. This is, in most cases, where the artist begins. Even when artists are illustrating their own work, they seldom create the pictures first and then write the text. Once we have some idea of the theme of the book, the motifs and moods, the characters, setting, and the events, we can go on to evaluate how well the artist has chosen artistic elements, principles, and conventions to convey those meanings visually, and how those artistic or stylistic choices have contributed to the overall aesthetic experience of the book.

It is interesting to note that in setting forth the criteria for awarding the Caldecott medal given for the most distinguished work of illustration published in the United States in a given year, the board of the Association of Library Services to Children (Peltola, 1980) suggests that

> each book is to be considered as a picture book. The committee is to make its decision primarily on the illustrations, but other components of a book are to be considered especially when they make a book less effective as a children's picture book. Such components might include the written text, the overall design of the book, etc. (p. 4)

I would argue that the written text and the design are integral parts of the picture book and must be evaluated along with the illustrations.

To a lesser extent perhaps, the critic must also keep in mind the "implied reader" (Iser, 1978) or viewer when evaluating the art of the picture book. Iser argues that there is always a negotiation of insight between the author (artist) and reader (viewer). It is in this co-construction of meaning that the illustrator of picture books invites the reader to participate. F. H. Langman (1967) suggested that to judge the effectiveness of the work, we must consider how the work itself "implies the kind of reader to whom it is addressed. . ." (p. 84). Thus, in evaluating a picture book, we may also need to consider the age and experience of the child who is the implied reader.

First and foremost, however, we must consider the range of choices available to the artist in expressing meaning. These stylistic choices can be categorized by the elements and principles of art, the technical choices relating to book production, and the historical and cultural conventions of depicting. In considering the range of these choices, we must consider not only their formal properties but also the ways in which they can add to the intellectual understanding and emotional engagement with the book.

THE ELEMENTS AND PRINCIPLES OF ART

While the elements and principles of art have been variously identified, line, shape, color, texture, and value are generally accepted as the basic elements with which the illustrator works. Under principles of organization, or the ways in which the artist brings these elements together, can be included compositional precepts such as eye movement, balance, rhythm, and pattern.

Line is the most commonly found element in picture books, perhaps because, as MacCann and Richard (1973) suggest, it is the "traditional mode of graphic illustration" (p. 36). Lines have great expressive potential. They can convey repose when horizontal, stability when vertical, and movement when diagonal. Angular lines can create a feeling of excitement or tension, while curving lines often express more rhythmic, peaceful qualities. The quality of line can be altered so that thin lines may appear fragile and delicate and thick lines can convey strength and weight.

We find the element of line effectively used to convey meaning in many picture books. In *Willie's Fire Engine,* for example, Charles Keeping (1980) uses contrasting thickness to set up a tension between his characters and their circumstances. His main characters are children trapped in an urban ghetto, perhaps with little hope of breaking out. Keeping draws them in thin, very delicate lines, suggesting fragility, but sets them in front of a black gate whose thick verticals resemble a set of prison bars. The diagonals become slashes across the page, crossing out any chance of escape. This is echoed in the lighter diagonals to the upper right, which form repeated x's and add further tension to the scene.

A very different use of line is found in *The Napping House* (Wood, 1984). Here, Don Wood uses short, thick vertical lines of a picket fence to suggest stable tranquillity. They are not frightening like Keeping's verticals because they are executed in softened shades of blue-white and because they are placed low on the page so as not to threaten. In covering the top of the fence with rose bushes, Wood creates an outline that suggests the rhythmic snoring of the sleepers first seen on the cover, as well as the soft curves of their bodies, and effectively leads the eye across the title and copyright pages. Without the curving line provided by the bushes, the picket fence would have ended in points, disturbing the quiet mood of the two pages.

When lines enclose space, as with the bushes in *The Napping House,* they create shapes, and as with line, the element of space is also capable of expressing meaning. Rounded or curving shapes are called biomorphic because they resemble living organisms. The circle in particular is a line endlessly meeting itself and thus symbolizes continuity and the eternal. Wood has used biomorphic shapes in *The Napping House* to convey a mood of tranquillity and gentle humor as well as the renewal found in restful sleep. The repetition of circles, ovals, and half circles throughout the book echoes the rhythm established in the early pages and also evokes circadian rhythms of biological life. There is not a sharp or a straight edge anywhere in the book to jar this effect; even the wooden furniture curves in defiance of reality.

Shapes with sharp edges and points, on the other hand, can convey excitement, action, tension, or even pain. Janina Domanska's use of abstracted, colorful shapes to retell *The Bremen Town Musicians* (Grimm, 1980) is a fine choice to convey the mournful quality of the animals' plight as each is threatened by illness or death. Later these shapes convincingly portray the nastiness of the robbers and the raucous victory of the animals as they trick these villains.

Mordicai Gerstein (1987) makes use of both geometric and biomorphic shapes in *The Mountains of Tibet*. To tell the life story of the Tibetan woodcutter, Gerstein places the pictures within squares, a perfect geometric shape, but like life, a square has sharp edges and points. When the woodcutter dies, however, the square changes to a circle, the universal symbol of eternity. Then he is presented with choices for another life, all enclosed within the shape of a circle. When he decides to return to the mountains of Tibet to live another life, he is reborn as a girl into a square-shaped picture. Gerstein artfully creates a metaphor for life and death that could never be expressed so powerfully with words alone.

The use of the element of shape can also create some interesting figure-ground relationships. Ann Jonas (1983) often works the background shapes in her two-dimensional pictorial spaces into major aspects of the design. This is particularly true in *Round Trip*, where the viewer must perceive the pure black and white shapes as either background or foreground and then switch when the book is turned upside-down. The interchange between the two is the essence of visual play in the book. Molly Bang (1980) takes this interplay of background and foreground shapes even further in *The Grey Lady and the Strawberry Snatcher*. Here the reversal of traditional shape or spatial relationships heightens the nightmare-like quality of the story. Moreover, the shapes formed by the larger areas of empty space set up lively tensions between the two characters.

Color is one of the most expressive of the elements. Colors can convey temperature (warm or cold) or emotion (red for anger or blue for melancholy). They are often associated with personality traits (purple for royalty, pink for femininity) and as such can lead to cultural stereotypes. In mainstream American culture, for example, the hero has often been portrayed in white and the villain in black. In addition, the intensity of a color (its brightness or dullness) as well as the ways in which colors are combined (color schemes) can also effect mood and evoke meaning.

For example, the early pictures in *Willie's Fire Engine* are dull brownish-gray, strengthening the dismal mood set up by Keeping's use of line. Later, however, as Willie's dream allows him to escape into the role of hero, Keeping shifts to bright reds and oranges. These colors not only represent the fire that Willie is rushing off to but also provide a glimpse of the heightened emotion of his inner feelings. Moreover, the change occurs at the very moment of climax of the story, and thus the colors underscore this literary element like a crash of cymbals in the finale of a symphony.

In *The Napping House,* Wood begins the story with a monochromatic color scheme, the use of single or closely related hues. The blues and purples of the early pages are further softened by the addition of gray, which adds to the restful mood of a gentle slumber. By the end of the book, however, when everyone is wakened by the restless flea, the scheme has changed to complementary, the use of colors opposite each other on the color wheel. The use of color complements not only makes each color appear brighter but also sends a burst of energy into the scene. Finally, on the end pages at the back of the book, the gray has been removed to produce a bright and cheerful robin's egg blue, as fully alive as a fresh spring morning.

In *The Napping House,* many will recognize the possible influence of Uri Shulevitz's (1974) *Dawn,* which used, to great effect, a similar movement from monochromatic to complementary scheme. In a later work, *Toddlecreek Post Office,* Shulevitz (1990) again manipulates color schemes effectively. The illustrations in this story about the loss of community have an overall blue tone made possible by specially tinted paper Shulevitz used for the original art. The blue anticipates the sad climax from the first pages, yet initially the addition of oranges and reds lends a sense of warmth to the scenes of life that center around a tiny village post office. When the postmistress who will close down this rural outpost arrives, however, suddenly the warm colors are removed leaving, cold, dark blues that chill our hearts.

Shulevitz's books also illustrate how contrast and mood can be manipulated in another way in art through the use of the element of value, the amount of light and dark tones. Value is easiest to recognize when illustrations are executed in black and white but is also a factor in illustrations executed in full color. When there is little contrast between light and dark, the mood of the picture may be either serene or brooding. Note, for example, Roger Duvoisin's *Hide and Seek Fog* (Tresselt, 1965) or Paul Zelinsky's *Hansel and Gretel* (Lesser, 1984).

On the other hand, with strong contrast between light and dark, the mood is often one of excitement or high drama. When value is used to define shapes, they take on a three-dimensional quality and become more lifelike. Lloyd Bloom's illustrations for Molly Chaffin's (1980) *We Be Warm Till Springtime Come* show how strongly contrasting values not only can breathe life into a picture but also can extend a message of warmth, even without color. In books such as *Jumanji*, Chris Van Allsburg (1981) uses contrasting values to convey the feeling that the pictures might actually get up and move off the page. Because our brain knows that the surface is two-dimensional, however, this factor heightens the touch of mystery or absurdity that seems to characterize Van Allsburg's work.

John Steptoe (1987) created strong contrast between light and dark in *Mufaro's Beautiful Daughters*. This contrast echoes the theme of opposites that is the essence of the story. Moreover, the contrasting values convey a sense of royal stature to the figures; in fact, the first view of the Prince whom Nyasha will marry almost looks like it was carved out of marble. Here the perfect male form further ennobles the people of whom Steptoe writes and links this great African civilization to the glories of ancient Greece.

In *Mufaro's Beautiful Daughters,* Steptoe also makes effective use of another element of art, the element of texture. Texture as an element is less noticeable in picture books because it can only be implied on the two-dimensional surface of the book's page. Steptoe artfully extends his theme of contrast between the two sisters and, more subtly, the contrast of id and ego within one personality by executing the illustrations in cross-hatching. This painstaking use of tiny lines in opposition to each other, often in opposing colors, characterizes all the drawings in the book and sets up a subtle feeling of movement or tension on each page. Moreover, Steptoe leaves areas of pure white on each double-page spread. Thus, the theme of contrasts is further reinforced by the contrast between the rough cross-hatching and the shiny, smooth whiteness of the book's paper.

In good picture books like these, no single element exists apart from the others. Rather, the illustrator will use principles of composition to unify elements on each page and on each succeeding page. In working with the arrangement of elements on each page, including the printed type, the artist will try to obtain an effective balance between unity and variety and to create certain visual patterns that may be carried on from page to page. Illustrators will try to ensure that the eye moves from one part of each double-page spread to another, both within the picture and between the picture and any printed text. This will in turn set up a subtle rhythm that can be carried on throughout the book. All of these choices can further express the visual meanings conveyed by the elements and contribute to a whole that is greater than the sum of its parts.

Charles Keeping has carefully considered these principles of design in *Willie's Fire Engine*. In the early pages of the book, the dullness of Willie's life is echoed in the layout of the pictures on the first two double-page spreads. On the left-hand page, we see a far shot of Willie's city with a golden castle far in the distance, out of his reach. On the facing page, we see a close-up of Willie's tenement building. As we turn the page, we see a picture of Willie inside in his room. On the right, we see Willie outdoors with the milkman, the only "hero" he knows. These four single pages set up a dull plodding echo that in their tones and use of line are reflections of the sameness of Willie's life. On the following pages, the two views are fragmented into four scenes and perhaps represent Willie's broken hopes. As Willie meets a girl who will help him on his quest, however, Keeping begins to vary the shapes and number of vignettes on each double-page spread, increasing the tension and action just as the colors begin to brighten and the lines to flow. The design of the book thus increases the emotional intensity almost unbearably until finally the brilliant reds of the fire engine burst across a double-page spread. Then the scenes once again get smaller and more numerous as the denouement occurs. The colors remain intense, however, and even when we see, on the last page, that Willie has been dreaming, the changed colors and subjects of the pictures on his wall provide a message of hope and seem to indicate that his dreams may enhance his life.

For Verna Aardema's (1981) retelling of *Bringing the Rain to Kapiti Plain*, Beatriz Vidal has used the principles of variety and unity to set up a visual pattern that echoes the verbal refrains of the text: "This is the great Kapiti Plain, all fresh and green from the African rains." The clear poetic beat of this cumulative tale is echoed and enlivened by Vidal's design. Beginning on the title page, she alternates the placement of blocks of type with cloud and earth images from left to right. To vary the symmetry of this pattern, however, she inserts a double spread where the shapes of cloud and earth enlarge to cover the entire two pages. Variations on this pattern are carried out through the book, adding interest to text and image that might otherwise have become too static. In addition, the visual rhythms set up in this way are so strong that they recall the beat of an African drum and further enhance the overall meaning and integrity of the book.

TECHNICAL CHOICES RELATING TO BOOK PRODUCTION

While the illustrator's choices of the elements and principles of art can have the most profound effect on the aesthetic experience we have with a given book, there are aspects of book production that can also convey subtle meanings and perhaps deepen that experience.

End pages, for example, are necessary in all books, but many artists use them as important introductions to the story. Paul Zelinsky created grandiose landscapes to provide the setting for a version of *Hansel and Gretel* (Lesser, 1984). These pictures pull the reader into his Renaissance setting immediately and then bring the story to closure. They provide a visual framing device that serves the same purpose as a "once upon a time" and "they lived happily ever after," the classic signals of narrative structure. In another approach, Nonny Hogrogian uses the end pages to highlight an important motif in her version of the Grimms' (1981a) *Cinderella.* She includes multiple views of a hazelnut twig, a gift from Cinderella's father that will grow on her mother's grave and provide the magic that transforms her life.

The artist's choice of original media may also affect the mood and validity of the book's theme. Although what we see in a picture book is a reproduction of the artist's finished work and should be evaluated as such (just as we evaluate an etching or lithograph and not the original metal plate or stone), the quality of the original media can enhance or interfere with visual meaning. In *Rain Rain Rivers,* for example, Shulevitz's (1969) choice of transparent watercolor echoes the book's title and theme and allows the white of the page to show through as if we were seeing light reflected in a rainy puddle. Van Allsburg's choice of conté pencil to execute the original pictures in *Jumanji* reproduces well and combines with the choice of a matte, rather rough paper stock in the book to convey an air of mysterious smokiness. We almost feel as if the pencil dust might rub off on our fingers as we touch the page, just as the game comes to life for the children.

We might compare two versions of the same tale to see how choice of original media changes the meaning of a book. In the 1968 edition of Jane Yolen's *Greyling,* a story set in and near the seas of Scotland, William Stobb's use of transparent paint conveys the watery realm of the selkie, or seal, transformed into human form. The flowing brush strokes allowed by the medium help to move the story along visually and heighten the stormy climax. In the 1991 version, David Ray has chosen acrylic paint, which he uses thickly, creating a texture that more closely resembles oil or oil pastels. While this medium gives more solid form to the seal turned human and provides a different visual emphasis to the story, it seems to turn the overall mood static. The watery forms are no longer fluid but seem changed into stone, and somehow the story loses its emotional impact.

Another technical choice that is unique to book production is the typeface in which the title and written text will be printed. Not only are the styles of typography important to the visual effect of the book but also the white spaces between the letters. Eric Carle's (1977) choice of a clean, sans serif type for *The Grouchy Lady Bug* echoes and balances the sharp edges of his cutout shapes. A more elaborate typography was chosen for Sidjakov's illustrations in *Baboushka and the Three Kings* (Robbins, 1960) and becomes part of the linear design of the book. In Fred Marcellino's version of *Puss in Boots* (Perrault, 1990), the typeface not only mirrors the ornate fussiness of a French court but also functions as part of the overall visual design through its size and color.

The artist's point of view can extend or heighten the overall meaning of the book. In many books, artists have used point of view like the lens of a camera to zoom in on subjects at emotional moments, as does Charles Keeping in *Willie's Fire Engine* or Donald Carrick (1981) in *Ben and the Porcupine*. Shulevitz moves the viewer from close-ups to long shots in *Dawn* in order to emphasize majestic views of the natural landscape. To relieve the sameness of repetition of verbal text and visual setting in *The Napping House,* Wood subtly moves the eye up the wall of the room so that eventually we are looking down on the scene from a bird's-eye view. Van Allsburg also changes perspective or point of view in *Jumanji* to add variety to what might have been visual monotony of pictures always placed on the right-hand page.

The artist's choice of pictorial content can be essential to the book's overall meaning and may be the most important of technical choices. While many artists may choose to represent or echo the verbal text of a book, the aesthetic experience is enhanced when the artist brings something extra to the scene. For example, in *Julius, The Baby of the World,* Kevin Henkes' (1990) illustrations add to the sense of contrast between the parent's love for the new baby brother and sister Lilly's jealousy. The pictures contradict the objective tone of the words and reflect Lilly's intense emotional feelings at the same time that they add a strong note of humor to the story, acknowledging the young child's right to those feelings and accepting them with warmth rather than rejection.

Julie Vivas' (1986) interpretation of *The Nativity* conveys a similar sense of warmth and wonder; a familiar yet often coldly formal verbal story is made at once human and personal when the characters are viewed through the naive but pure eyes of a child. On the other hand, Trina Schart Hyman brings psychological darkness to her version of *Snow White* (Grimm, 1974) by showing the young and voluptuous stepmother's descent into madness. The familiar tale becomes entirely new through Hyman's pictorial choices, including the objects in the rooms and the faces on the magic mirror.

Comparing Hyman's version of *Snow White* to Nancy Burkert's illustrations (Grimm, 1972) shows how pictorial content and point of view can combine to convey very different meanings. For example, while

Hyman fully develops the character of the stepmother through the pictures, Nancy Burkert never shows us the stepmother's face. Moreover, in Hyman's version, we are immediately drawn into the tale with dark, flowing lines and shapes. In our first view of Snow White's mother, we are in the room with her as she pricks her finger, the red drops of blood visible on the snow on the window sill. Burkert's version begins much more formally. Regular, geometric shapes on the end pages convey a feeling of stately objectivity, as does the rectangular shape of the mirror placed squarely in the middle of the title page. In this version, we see Snow White's mother from outside the castle, and while she may have pricked her finger, we have no visual evidence of blood. Thus, we are safely distanced from the emotional intensity of the story. Unlike Hyman's version, which becomes a story of mother-daughter conflict resulting in the utter downfall of an evil personality through her own failings, Burkert gives us the story of an innocent child whose escape from evil is brought about by others. Both versions are powerful in their own ways, and both show how far beyond the verbal elements of text an artist can bring us.

HISTORICAL AND CULTURAL CONVENTIONS

The last category of stylistic choices available to an artist concerns the pictorial conventions associated with particular times or peoples. In the past, reviewers have attempted to categorize the art of today's picture books according to accepted categories of art history, such as realism, impressionism, or nonobjective art. This does little to extend our understanding of a book's quality or of how the artist has chosen to express meaning. Moreover, picture books do not always fit neatly into these pictorial categories. However, if we recall Novitz's (1976) suggestion that certain pictorial conventions are accepted as procedures for depicting, we might look at these umbrella conventions, be they historical or cultural, as another range of choices available to the illustrator for expressing meaning.

For example, early Christian art is characterized by the need for a clear, uniform message to a mostly illiterate audience. This need to convey readily recognized symbols and motifs transcended individualistic portrayals. Many illustrators have thus chosen conventions from this historical period to convey stories and songs associated with this broad time period. Janina Domanska (1975) echoes the stained glass windows of Romanesque churches to bring the Christmas carol *Din Dan Don It's Christmas* to book form. Juan Wijngaard, in *Sir Gawain and the Loathly Lady* (Hastings, 1985), and Trina Schart Hyman, in *St. George and the Dragon* (Hodges, 1984), have both used conventions of illuminated manuscripts to bring ancient tales to life by associating the time of the original tales with the art of that period.

We can find similar use of a broad range of historical conventions chosen effectively by many picture book illustrators, from Paul Zelinsky's borrowing of Renaissance trends toward dramatic lighting and emphasis on form and space to retell *Hansel and Gretel*, to Anthony Browne's use of conventions of surrealism to convey his psychologically deep stories (Grimm, 1981b).

Other artists may borrow conventions that have come to be associated with particular cultures over time. Thus Paul Goble makes use of styles found in the buffalo hide paintings of Northern Plains Indians to retell their legends and tales. Likewise, in their stories with Chinese or Asian settings or roots, Ed Young (Louie, 1982) and Demi (1991) have effectively used techniques of Chinese art, which is characterized by the exploration of linear effects and the de-emphasis of realism.

In all these cases, the theme of the book, its setting in time and place, and its overall effect is strengthened by the artist's choice of certain historical or cultural conventions. We must judge the book not as to whether the illustrations match the definition of a particular period or culture but as to whether the artist has chosen those elements that enhance and extend the meaning of the book for today's reader.

CONCLUSION

Here then is a theory of visual criticism, based on understandings from the field of aesthetics and art criticism, that lends itself to evaluating picture books. The theory grows out of a firm belief that we must understand how the illustrator chooses to convey meaning, and it seeks to explore or categorize the range of choices possible for illustrators of picture books in accomplishing that task. This theory can form the basis for further exploration of the art in picture books through fine works such as Joseph Schwarcz's (1982) *Ways of the Illustrator* and *The Picture Book Comes of Age* (Schwarcz & Schwarcz, 1990), Perry Nodleman's (1988) *Words about Pictures,* or Molly Bang's (1991) *Picture This.* These and other books are particularly useful for understanding the works of selected illustrators in greater depth.

Understanding the art of the picture book in terms of stylistic choices can provide a useful basis for looking at children's responses to the art of the picture book. My own research with children has indicated that in classrooms where teachers provide many opportunities for looking at picture books and for responding to them in a variety of ways, children seem to move naturally toward understanding that the artist's choices are meant to convey visual meaning and that these choices evoke an emotional response. Children also seem to be capable of identifying more universal conventions of art in their own terms, classifying Sendak's (1981) illustrations for *Outside Over There*, for example, as "from the bible" or "lushy" and Van Allsburg's pictures as "like clay" or "like stone" (Kiefer, 1986).

Langer (1953) has argued that artwork is an expression of the artist's idea,

> i.e. something that takes shape as he articulates an envisagement of realities which discursive language cannot properly express. What he makes is a symbol—primarily a symbol to capture and hold his own imagination of organized feeling, the rhythms of life, the forms of emotion. (p. 392)

I believe it is this powerful quality of the visual art of the picture book that gives rise to the deepest responses on the part of all readers, adults or children. Thus, the visual expression of meaning and the resulting emotional experience made possible by that expression should be paramount in evaluating picture books. When the right choices are made by the artist, children of all ages will bring, in response, their own understandings to the work in ways that will not only develop their visual literacy but will also deepen their aesthetic understanding.

APPENDIX

THE ARTIST'S CHOICES IN EXPRESSING MEANING: CRITERIA FOR EVALUATING PICTURE BOOKS

Design Choices

1. The *elements* of design (line, shape, color, value, and texture) are chosen for their expressive qualities.
   - Lines and shapes convey action, rhythm; they can be strong and solid or diminutive and quick.
   - Colors convey mood, emotions.
   - Value creates contrast, highly dramatic or soothing effects.
   - Texture conveys tension, adds interest or movement.
2. The *principles* of design or composition (balance, rhythm, repetition, variety in unity, eye movement) are chosen to tie individual pages into a complete whole that reinforces the overall meaning of the book.
   - Layout and size of pictures carry the eye from page to page and create a rhythm in keeping with the meaning of the book.
   - Pictures and printed text are well balanced and create a pleasing pattern.
   - Elements of design are used to create variety in unity.

Technical Choices

1. Original media, end papers, paper stock, and typography are chosen to strengthen ideas or story.
   - Choice of watercolor, acrylics, pencil, or print is in keeping with the mood of the story or concept.
   - Typeface appropriate to type of book or story.
   - End papers prepare the reader by setting the mood, giving a preview, or complementing the illustrations.
   - The paper itself is in keeping with original media (acrylic on shiny paper, watercolor or pencil on a matte finish).
2. Pictorial content and the artist's point of view extend and enhance the story or concept.
   - Choice of what to include in the picture is appropriate to the story and adds new dimensions, new or additional meanings.
   - Pictures add information and help us see ideas in new ways.
   - Close-ups, traditional perspective, worm's-eye view, or bird's-eye view are chosen to lend excitement, drama, and interest to the story.

Choices of Historical or Cultural Conventions

1. Pictorial conventions are borrowed from styles of art throughout history to enhance and extend the meaning of the story or concept.
   - Aspects of early Christian art, Renaissance painting, French impressionism, etc., are used to convey mood and meaning.
2. Pictorial conventions are borrowed from particular cultural groups to enhance meaning.
   - Folk motifs or styles lend authenticity to tales, poems, or concepts related to particular cultures.

REFERENCES

Aardema, V. (1981). *Bringing the rain to Kapiti Plain: A Nandi tale*. Illustrated by B. Vidal. New York: Dial.

Bader, B. (1976). *American picture books: From Noah's ark to the beast within*. New York: Macmillan.

Bang, M. (1980). *The grey lady and the strawberry snatcher*. New York: Four Winds Press.

Bang, M. (1991). *Picture this: Perception and composition*. Boston, MA: Little, Brown.

Carle, E. (1977). *The grouchy ladybug*. New York: Crowell.

Carrick, C. (1981). *Ben and the porcupine*. Illustrated by D. Carrick. New York: Clarion Books.

Chaffin, L. D. (1980). *We be warm till springtime come*. Illustrated by L. Bloom. New York: Macmillan.

Demi. (1991). *Chingis Khan*. New York: Holt.

Domanska, J. (1975). *Din dan don it's Christmas*. New York: Greenwillow Books.

Genova, J. (1979). The significance of style. *Journal of Aesthetics and Art Criticism*, *37*(3), 315-324.

Gerstein, M. (1987). *The mountains of Tibet*. New York: Harper & Row.

Golden, J. (1990). *The narrative symbol in children's literature: Explorations of the construction of text*. New York: Mouton de Gruyer.

Gombrich, E. H. (1982). *The image and the eye: Further studies in the psychology of pictorial representation*. Ithaca, NY: Cornell University Press.

Grimm, J. (1972). *Snow-white and the seven dwarfs* (R. Jarrell, Trans.). Illustrated by N. Burkert. New York: Farrar, Straus, and Giroux.

Grimm, J. (1974). *Snow White* (P. Heins, Trans.). Illustrated by T. S. Hyman. Boston, MA: Little, Brown.

Grimm, J. (1980). *The Bremen town musicians* (E. Shub, Trans.). Illustrated by J. Domanska. New York: Greenwillow Books.

Grimm, J. (1981a). *Cinderella*. Illustrated by N. Hogrogian. New York: Greenwillow Books.

Grimm, J. (1981b). *Hansel and Gretel*. Illustrated by A. Browne. New York: Franklin Watts.

Hastings, S. (1985). *Sir Gawain and the loathly lady*. Illustrated by J. Wijngaard. New York: Lothrop, Lee & Shepard.

Hellman, G. (1977). Symbol systems and artistic styles. *Journal of Aesthetics and Art Criticism*, *35*(3), 279-292.

Henkes, K. (1990). *Julius, The baby of the world*. New York: Greenwillow Books.

Hodges, M. (1984). *St. George and the dragon*. Illustrated by T. S. Hyman. Boston, MA: Little, Brown.

Hutchins, P. (1971). *Titch*. New York: Macmillan.

Iser, W. (1978). *The act of reading: A theory of aesthetic response*. Baltimore, MD: Johns Hopkins University Press.

Jonas, A. (1983). *Round trip*. New York: Greenwillow Books.

Keeping, C. (1980). *Willie's fire engine*. New York: Oxford University Press.

Kiefer, B. (1986). The child and the picture book: Creating live circuits. *Children's Literature Association Quarterly*, *11*(2), 63-68.

Kiefer, B. (1989). Picture books for all the ages. In J. Hickman & B. E. Cullinan (Eds.), *Children's literature in the classroom: Weaving Charlotte's web* (pp. 75-88). Needham Heights, MA: Christopher-Gordon Publishers.

Langer, S. K. (1942). *Philosophy in a new key: A study in the symbolism of reason, rite, and art*. Cambridge MA: Harvard University Press.

Langer, S. K. (1953). *Feeling and form*. New York: Scribner.

Langman, F. H. (1967). The idea of the reader in literary criticism. *British Journal of Aesthetics*, *7*(1), 81-87.

Lesser, R. (1984). *Hansel and Gretel*. Illustrated by P. Zelinsky. New York: Dodd, Mead.

Louie, A. (1982). *Yeh-shen: A Cinderella story from China*. Illustrated by E. Young. New York: Philomel Books.

MacCann, D., & Richard, O. (1973). *The child's first books: A critical study of pictures and text.* New York: H. W. Wilson.

Marantz, K. (1977). The picture book as art object: A call for balanced reviewing. *Wilson Library Bulletin, 52*(2), 148-151.

Nodelman, P. (1988). *Words about pictures: The narrative art of children's picture books.* Athens, GA: University of Georgia Press.

Novitz, D. (1976). Conventions and the growth of pictorial style. *British Journal of Aesthetics, 16*(4), 324-337.

Peltola, B. (1980). *Caldecott award committee manual.* Chicago, IL: Association of Library Services to Children.

Perrault, C. (1990). *Puss in Boots* (M. Arthur, Trans.). Illustrated by F. Marcellino. New York: Farrar, Straus, and Giroux.

Robbins, R. (1960). *Baboushka and the three kings.* Illustrated by N. Sidjakov. Berkeley, CA: Parnassus Press.

Schwarcz, J. H. (1982). *Ways of the illustrator.* Chicago, IL: American Library Association.

Schwarcz, J. H., & Schwarcz, C. (1990). *The picture book comes of age: Looking at childhood through the art of illustration.* Chicago, IL: American Library Association.

Sendak, M. (1981). *Outside over there.* New York: Harper & Row.

Shulevitz, U. (1969). *Rain rain rivers.* New York: Farrar, Straus, and Giroux.

Shulevitz, U. (1974). *Dawn.* New York: Farrar, Straus, and Giroux.

Shulevitz, U. (1990). *Toddlecreek post office.* New York: Farrar, Straus, and Giroux.

Steig, W. (1982). *Dr. DeSoto.* New York: Farrar, Straus, and Giroux.

Steptoe, J. (1987). *Mufaro's beautiful daughters: An African tale.* New York: Lothrop, Lee & Shepard.

Tresselt, A. R. (1965). *Hide and seek fog.* Illustrated by R. Duvoisin. New York: Lothrop, Lee & Shepard.

Van Allsburg, C. (1981). *Jumanji.* Boston, MA: Houghton Mifflin.

Vivas, J. (1986). *The Nativity.* San Diego, CA: Gulliver Books.

Wolfflin, H. (1932). *Principles of art history* (M. Hottinger, Trans.). New York: Dorer Publications.

Wood, A. (1984). *The napping house.* Illustrated by D. Wood. San Diego, CA: Harcourt Brace Jovanovich.

Yolen, J. (1968). *Greyling.* Illustrated by W. Stobbs. New York: World Publishing.

Yolen, J. (1991). *Greyling.* Illustrated by D. Ray. New York: Philomel Books.

CATHRYN M. MERCIER

Assistant Professor
Associate Director
Center for the Study of Children's Literature
Simmons College
Boston, Massachusetts

Insights and Discoveries: Illuminating Textual Criticism

INTRODUCTION

Textual criticism—two simple words that present a host of challenges. The topic immediately introduces the problems of relationship and emphasis. What arcane relationship connects these two words? Does textual criticism mean literary criticism? What roles does critical theory play in the practice, process, and products of criticism? And what roles does it play in the evaluation of children's books? *Textual* comes before *criticism,* so does focus fall on the text? Or, since *textual* modifies *criticism,* perhaps criticism should ground the discussion.

CRITICISM AND CHILDREN'S LITERATURE

Where you place the emphasis reveals a great deal about you as a reader and as a critic. Many a critic of children's literature would find text the appropriate place to begin:

> Criticism that does not deal with the text is worthless. It may be useful as history or biography and, indeed, critics often dally along some rather peculiar paths; but criticism disqualifies itself as criticism if it does not deal directly with the text.
>   The first law of the critical jungle, therefore, should be "Loyalty to the Text." (Kingsbury, 1984, p. 18)

Paul Heins (1970b) keeps company with this primary placement of the text. He questions those who champion child appeal as most crucial:

Interestingly enough, John Rowe Townsend looks upon "acceptability to a child as a preliminary hurdle rather than a final test." Personally, I question whether Mr. Townsend has not put the cart before the horse. In discussions of recently published children's books, generally after a discussion of a book of rare value, one often hears the voice of the devil's advocate: "But, will children like it?" or more pessimistically, "What child will read it?" Surely the question of acceptability to a child is a question concerning book selection and not a fundamental critical question—not a question of literary criticism. (p. 270)

Underlying a textual focus may be the "most insidious and dangerous of critical . . . misconceptions: that a story has a single meaning" (Hunt, 1984-85, p. 191). The assumption that adults can determine that meaning and then communicate it to children persists as even more insidious. After all, children couldn't possibly discover that meaning themselves, could they? And where would we be if they did? It's that attitude which scares me and causes my hesitancy to position "textual" solely at the nexus of my critical approach. True, life-experienced and reading-experienced adults bring knowledge to a text, but can we afford to imbue their reading with greater seriousness— with greater value—than a child's reading? Can we risk acting as if children don't read critically? Believing that children and adults read differently, and recognizing the awkwardness of adults reading literature directed at the child audience, Peter Hunt (1991) calls for a childist approach to criticism. It would

involve a total re-reading of texts. . . . Simply to invite adults to read as children is scarcely novel, and it is likely not only to revive old prejudices, but, as we have seen, to prove remarkably difficult. Rather, we have to challenge all our assumptions, question every reaction, and ask what reading as a child actually means, given the complexities of the cultural interaction. (p. 191)

Basic to Hunt's concept is the belief that a child reads differently, not simply, not less effectively, nor less intelligently; the critic should not confuse a childist with a child-like reading (Hunt, 1991). Speculating on what the term "children's literature" means may expose ways in which "reading children's literature is, for the adult, a more complex process than reading an adult book" (Hunt, 1991, p. 45). Nearly every textbook, every special section of a journal, every guide to research and theory in the field, attempts to articulate a manageable and practical definition of children's literature. In his lucid and insightful book *Criticism, Theory, and Children's Literature,* Hunt (1991) devotes an entire chapter to this activity and considers the complex value judgments implicit in naming any book as "literature." The very word suggests not just good, but the best—genuine excellence. His chapter concludes by asking for a definition of child because "children's literature, in separating itself (for administrative convenience), defines itself in terms (uniquely) of its audience" (p. 56):

All of this suggests a species of literature defined in terms of the reader
rather than the authors' intentions or the texts themselves. It also
demonstrates the closeness of the relationship between the text and the reader,
and, consequently, the peculiar honesty and realism required of the children's
book critic. (p. 1)

This "peculiar honesty and realism required of the children's book
critic" turns my discussion to the relationship between text and critic,
therefore to a consideration of criticism.

THE ROLE OF CRITICISM

If "criticism" is the emphasis, then the activity (criticism) takes
precedence over its subject (the text). What inherent assumptions does
that perspective carry? It supposes that the activity of literary criticism,
of thinking and writing about literature, has a purpose and a merit
which extend beyond the literature itself. Further, it implies that criticism
can yield a product or products and that those products themselves
deserve attention. By extension, the products may even take precedence
over the original subject: the text. We read criticism about books, not
the books themselves. Paul Heins (1970b) believes that "every time we
pass judgment on a book or express enthusiasm for it, we are engaging
in a critical act" (p. 265). Therefore, reviews and annotations are one
act of criticism. Criticism also generates longer pieces, developed articles
and books that examine a specific genre, author, or work or group
of works from an individual vantage point. Still, the criticism here
revolves around a specific text or sets of texts.

Textual criticism often yields additional criticism in the form of
written responses and defenses, the apologetics of children's literature.
"Just as romantic poets and realistic novelists have had in the past
to defend their positions, just as fiction itself and drama have had to
withstand puritanical and other kinds of religious attacks and criticism,
children's literature . . . needs constant defending" (Heins, 1970a, p.
372). While justification lies at the roots of apologetics, construction
of a defense can prove liberating and illuminating to writer and reader.
It presents an opportunity to sharpen some axes a critic may be grinding
(Kingsbury, 1984, p. 20) and to realize how they dull with lack of use
or how they may need to be exchanged for more advanced instruments.
Apologetics offer an opportunity to affirm and to change attitudes,
to move children's literature from considerations of practice and
pragmatics into persuasive, philosophical discussions as well. The
dialogue can heighten awareness of the creativity, artistry, and excellence
in children's literature and prove it a field for rich exploration and
original work. In one influential apologetic, John Rowe Townsend

(1971) demonstrates the absurdity of an anti-intellectual view of children's literature:

> The few to whom children's literature is central cannot expect, within one working lifetime, to master sufficient knowledge of the related fields [e.g., psychology, linguistics, sociology, history] to meet the experts on their own ground and at their own level. And yet, while the children's literature person obviously cannot operate at a professional level in all these various fields, the people operating in the various fields can and quite properly do take an interest in children's reading as it affects their own specialities, and are able to quite frequently pronounce upon it. But, understandably, such people are often unaware of or have not thought deeply about the aspects of children's literature that do *not* impinge upon their own field. The subject is one on which people are notoriously willing to pronounce with great confidence but rather little knowledge. Consequently, we have a flow of apparently authoritative comment by people who are undoubtedly experts but who are not actually experts on *this*. (pp. 375-376)

Avi (1986) makes the same point anecdotally:

> A recent fiction review for the New York *Times* appeared with this credit line: ". . . lives in Vermont and writes about national security issues." In his review, this reviewer concluded by saying, "But maybe, living in Vermont, I just don't understand the reading habits of children, the requirements of libraries, or the business of publishing." *I* say, why blame Vermont? (p. 115)

Avi implies another possibility of criticism, one which Virginia Woolf (1939) also explored. These authors look to criticism for serious, informed commentary about art—their art. Woolf goes so far as to propose a system that generates a consultation between a reviewer and an author, "bring[ing] both parties together in a union that is profitable, to the minds and purses of both . . . [giving the author] the advantage of coming into touch with a well-stored mind, housing other books and even other literatures. . . ." (pp. 20-21). If criticism affects the artist, then it also affects the future of art itself. Thus, there exists a real possibility that one product of criticism just may be to challenge writers to push the artistic boundaries of literature.

Peter Hunt (1984-85) asserts that "wherever you look, there seems to be an inevitable link between children's literature and modern criticism" (p. 191). Theorizing results when readers of criticism and critics themselves reflect on their work. It's a self-reflexive process. In challenging each other, these readers question each others'—and their own—driving assumptions. What basic beliefs, attitudes, and values operate beneath a given critical statement or critical act? On what inclusions does criticism depend? What does it exclude? "Theory is an uncomfortable and uncomforting thing, for by seeking to explain what we might have thought was obvious, it draws attention to some of the hidden problems. . . . Theory may not solve any of these problems directly, but it forces us to confront them" (Hunt, 1984-85, p. 191). Additionally, participation in critical theory can "extricate children's literature from the narrow boundaries of the past and to place it in the foreground of literary scholarship, facing the future" (Shavit, 1986, p. x). While this last statement sounds simultaneously deprecating and ambitious, it does recognize the marginalization of children's literature, and therefore of children themselves (and all who work with and on behalf of children), as it avows the potential of children's literature to enlighten other literatures, other texts, other criticisms.

Skimming the table of contents in the June 1990 *The Lion and the Unicorn* proves this point. The issue's theme is "Politics and Ideology"—note, not "the politics of the playground" or "ideologies evident in the nursery" but something fuller, more expansive. It features articles such as "Taking Political Stock: New Theoretical and Critical Approaches to Anglo-American Children's Literature in the 1980s," "History and the Politics of Play in T. S. Eliot's 'The Burial of the Dead' and Arthur Ransome's *Swallows and Amazons*," "Children of the Revolution: A Literary Case Study," and "From Little Black Sambo to Popo and Fifina: Arna Bontemps and the Creation of African-American Children's Literature" (Politics and ideology, 1990, p. 5). If these long titles, complete with their telltale scholarly colons, weren't enough to put such essays within the academic arena, their perceptive, original, and cogent arguments would serve as models for others. On a similar note, the Modern Language Association recently published *Teaching Children's Literature: Issues, Pedagogy, Resources* (Sadler, 1992) as one of its "Options for Teaching" series intended for college and university instructors. Children's literature keeps company in this series with other theoretical considerations of curriculum, study, and methods. The introduction to the volume states:

> Although the dismissal of "kiddie lit" has certainly abated in academic circles in recent years, the segregation of children's literature seems to persist as much as before, even though attention to its texts should be of enormous concern to the student of "adult" classics. . . .
>
> Literary historians, too, might benefit from a closer look at the relation between child texts and adult texts. . . .
>
> We will have to go beyond the parochial (or territorial) attitudes responsible for [this] segregation. . . . [to overcome] those who still welcome the isolation of a field once confined to schools of education, who continue to regard the study of child texts as a less demanding and less rigorous enterprise. . . . submissions of essays to journals [devoted to children's literature continue] . . . as more and more serious articles in children's literature appear in these journals, as well as in *PMLA* [*Publications of the Modern Language Association*], *ELH, Nineteenth-Century Literature* and *Critical Inquiry*, the standards (and stakes) are steadily raised. (Knoepflmacher, 1992, pp. 3-5)

LITERARY THEORY

But what is the role of theory in textual criticism? Kay Vandergrift (1990) finds that "the purpose of . . . theory is to bring readers closer to literary works" (p. 1). As an outcome of criticism, the most valuable contribution that theory makes seems basic. Like criticism, theory offers occasion for illumination. Exposure to and consideration of critical theories can initiate reflection on ways of reading and thinking about books and can foster greater knowledge about ourselves as readers and as critics—as readers of literature but also as readers of criticism. Vandergrift (1990) views theory as a metaphor and warns:

> Keep in mind that all theories are themselves products of the imagination. . . . Literary theory, therefore, is a metaphor about metaphors. Theories are fictions without the full strength of "make believe" engendered by a fictional work of art, but, nonetheless, they are fictions which may lead to insight and discovery. (p. 1)

Insight and discovery: the two final, hard-won, desirable products of criticism. In trying on different theoretical personas, one can follow new paths to perspicacity about a given book. Furthermore, having a range of theoretical lenses enables one to be a knowledgeable consumer of criticism; to read reviews with discernment of the reviewer's precarious location "out on a limb" (Heins, 1970b, p. 264) but also with a cognizance of the reviewer's possible biases and critical approach; to read collections of essays about literature with an experienced eye and a practiced mind; and to participate in debates about children's literature in an open, confident way. Ultimately, exploring a variety of critical theories may lead one to recognize her own agendas, to see what critical axes she may be grinding and why.

Criticism needn't be negative; perhaps it needn't even be judgmental. To earn the title, the critic cannot function only as another reader, albeit a better one (Heins, Townsend, Hunt); he must also embrace the responsibility to offer fresh perspectives. The critic stands obligated to give a thoughtful reading of the text and to provide an expansive vision of it, not always to show what the text does not do, but to explore what it does and what promise it exhibits.

How does one demonstrate this illuminating potential of criticism? One could attempt to trace critical theory in the practice of reviewing. In doing so, one could sample book reviews currently available and consider them in terms of what theoretical influences appear in them. That exercise is based on two arrogant assumptions: one, that the reviewer wrote directly out of a theoretical framework; and two, that theoretical principles of criticism direct the review more than attention to audience or to text does.

One could examine a single text, one well known to a general audience. Then, one could overlay this textual base with an assortment of theoretical transparencies. While this strategy holds tantalizing appeal, it falsely assumes that each theoretical gauze exposes a single meaning; for example, that a feminist approach will yield *one* way of reading that text. In fact, theory shifts the frame of critical vision; it works against a static interpretation as it allows the reader/critic to adopt a variety of ideologies with any given reading and with any given text. Further, to apply diverse theories to a single text, one must select the text. Heins presents that very selection as a critical act, so the exercise of theory will have influenced that decision. Even more problematic, though, stand the concealed values and judgments in the selection itself. From what element of literature does one choose? Does the choice come from historical children's literature? From contemporary books? In choosing, should one try to define a canon of children's literature? Ideally, each "school" of critical thought can explore every text with precision and elaboration, so how does one justify a particular text? And to change texts based on the theoretical frame threatens to result in easy correspondences rather than genuine illumination. For example, one could choose an archetypal reading of *The Wizard of Oz* focusing on the elements of Dorothy's quest, her journey from home and return—aspects obvious within the text and helpful in making a point quickly. However, a Marxist or a reader response interpretation could be more challenging to develop and could be uniquely penetrating and rich.

In "Enigma Variations: What Feminist Theory Knows about Children's Literature," Lissa Paul (1987) discusses a historical text, *The Secret Garden*, and a contemporary text, Margaret Mahy's (1984) *The Changeover: A Supernatural Romance*, through feminist poetics. In the process, she realizes her own dissatisfaction with the shift away from Mary as Burnett's central character and the emergence of Colin as hero; she shows Mahy's effective use of the popularity of the romance novel to texture the character of Sorry Carlisle, to imbue him with qualities stereotypically ascribed to women, and to enable him to serve as guide to Laura on her journey to heroism. Paul's most extraordinary achievement, though, is this idea: "There is good reason for appropriating feminist theory to children's literature. Both women's literature and children's literature are devalued and regarded as marginal or peripheral by the literary and educational communities" (p. 187).

Feminism and Marxism share the common ground of oppression in their theoretical foundations. While it may be argued that Marxist criticism belongs under the umbrella of sociological criticism or of political criticism, its fastidious emphasis on economic power, on the Marxian concept of the dialectics of history, and on the revolutionary potential of literature carve out a unique niche. Jerry Phillips and Ian Wojcik-Andrews (1990b), in "Notes toward a Marxist Critical Practice," suggest that the critic/reader must "[open] a dialogue within the text between the historical condition of its production and the moment of its reception" (p. 127). That is, in fact, just what they do in the aforementioned piece on Eliot and Ransome published in *The Lion and the Unicorn* (Phillips & Wojcik-Andrews, 1990a).

Psychoanalytic criticism refers to a different sort of oppression, to repression, in its view of literature. It moves away from a new critic's attempt to view the text scientifically as a way of unlocking literary meaning and turns to analysis of the characters, their motives and operation within the text. Mary Lou White (1976) includes four articles on a psychological approach via "character analysis." Roni Natov (1990) combines a feminist and a psychoanalytical overlay in considering "Mothers and Daughters: Jamaica Kincaid's Pre-Oedipal Narrative." Here, she not only sheds light on the adolescent ambivalence of the title character, Annie John, toward her mother, but also touches on possible connections to the author's own experience.

White (1976) identifies biographical criticism as a subset of psychological criticism. Biocritical studies, such as the Twayne series about young adult authors which began with Patricia Campbell's (1985) *Presenting Robert Cormier,* strive to consider the fiction in the context of its creator, his intentions, and his life.

Archetypal critics are active in children's literature probably because of the dominating presence of folklore and fairy tales. Archetypal theory addresses the mythic and folkloric patterns evident in fiction, more often in fantasy but also in realism. Ursula Le Guin's (1979) "The Child and the Shadow" articulates her view of the Jungian archetype of shadow as it appears in literature, from Hans Christian Andersen to her own fantasy. The article itself serves as guide to reading Le Guin's (1968) archetype-rich novel *A Wizard of Earthsea,* in which Ged must face, name, and claim his own shadow in order to be whole. Natalie Babbitt's (1987) "Fantasy and the Classic Hero" both celebrates and bemoans her unknowing return to and employment of Joseph Campbell's archetypal heroic journey. Babbitt outlines the separation-initiation-return model in a handful of children's books and discusses the other necessary elements to make the literary hero's journey a successful one. She concludes affirming the inevitability of the motif:

> The total round of the hero's path is vitally important. Without it we cannot tell stories that satisfy us. . . . To carry on in that tradition, to take the hero through his round and bring him home again, over and over, is an ancient and honorable exercise that will never lose its vitality or its value. It has always existed somewhere in literature. . . . (p. 155)

The Children's Literature Association Quarterly (Moss, 1982) devoted a special section to essays on a structuralist response to children's literature. "Literary structuralists believe that literature is non-referential; they neither discover meaning nor assign meaning to a work, but attempt to identify how one uses various semiotic conventions in making sense of texts" (Vandergrift, 1990, p. 15). In pursuing a structuralist chain of exposition, Stephen Roxburgh (1982) isolates the visual and textual elements of *Anno's Counting Book* (Anno, 1977) and unfolds the layers of visual and textual elements which build to develop meaning in the picture book. Jonathan Stott (1987) applies structuralist concepts to a classroom situation. He drives toward understanding ways in which children become proficient readers as they master the symbolic structures of stories. Literary works read and discussed in school "become increasingly more complex in their uses of the various elements of the literary codes" (p. 153), and Stott describes ways in which "each work becomes a building block in the foundation on which increased literary understanding is built" (p. 153).

Reader response critics place the text in a secondary position and focus attention on the reader. Aidan Chambers (1983) writes, "as we read our whole lives—our personal histories—are open to the book and can be engaged, can be brought to memory, by features in the book. . . ." (p. 176). This activity includes life experiences and reading experiences. Ever aware of educational practicality, though simultaneously appreciative of the complexity of its implementation, Chambers maps "a critical blueprint" (p. 174).

Peter Hunt's (1990) call for a "childist" approach to criticism of children's literature exhibits a reader response bias. However, Hunt's advocacy of a childist poetics exerts an even greater demand on adult critics, challenging them to acknowledge the baggage they bring to the text and to strive to discard some of it as they endeavor to enter the text with an uncluttered attitude, yet one open to and aware of the culture of childhood.

In a 1990 cultural pluralism column in *The Children's Literature Association Quarterly,* Opal Moore and Donnarae MacCann (1990) employ a Black Aesthetic framework in writing "On Canon Expansion and the Artistry of Joyce Hansen." As do feminists, they focus on writers who have been ignored, undervalued, or devalued by mainstream criticism, and pay genuine critical attention to the work of those writers. They reveal Hansen as "establishing an historical and ethical context for the young within which they can interpret and respond more positively to the circumstances of their present lives" (p. 37). Based on "general principles of inclusion and empowerment" (p. 33), this theoretical application proves crucial for all readers, not only the excluded.

In discussing new historicism and its use in college English classrooms, Brook Thomas (1987) charges American culture, and therefore critical theory, with amnesia (p. 509) and calls for examining literature within a historical context. "A product of the past, forever capable of reproduction in the present, literature can help create a historical consciousness that reflects upon and judges our present situation. . . ." (p. 521). Thomas (1989) puts this theory to practice in "Preserving and Keeping Order by Killing Time in *Heart of Darkness*" where he moves from general ideas about history to their enlightenment of the text. He begins by naming Conrad "a historian of human experience" (p. 237) and concludes with having stripped the novel "from the cloak of time . . . to imagine a radically different form of temporal narrative" (pp. 254-255).

Geoff Moss (1990) considers the presence and success of metafiction, fiction about fiction, in children's literature, while David Lewis (1990) uses the conceits of self-conscious, self-reflexive fiction to elucidate the picture book:

> The metafictive in picture books can now be seen as an extreme and exaggerated manifestation of a tendency already deeply rooted in the form itself. By its nature, the picture book tends towards openness, the playful, the parodic—fertile ground in which the metafictive can flourish (p. 143).

New books, such as Jon Scieszka and Lane Smith's (1992) *The Stinky Cheese Man and Other Fairly Stupid Tales*, dramatically indulge this playfulness. Story, text, design, author and illustrator's biographies, cover art, and flap copy don't escape self-comment and manipulation. The sheer narcissism delights a reader.

And a final lens: deconstruction, which has been somewhat tardy in attending children's literature criticism until relatively recently. In fact, art in picture books such as *The Jolly Postman* by Janet and Allan Ahlberg (1986) operates successfully via the deconstructive idea of intertextual game playing. Avi's (1991) young adult novel *Nothing but the Truth* requires the reader to construct the narrative by frequently dislocating the reader (every time you think you know where you are, who's speaking, what's happening, either place, speakers, event, or document shifts). One aspect of deconstruction, this dislocation, connects to another as the text forces the reader to attend to the role of gaps and silences as generative of meaning within the novel.

CONCLUSION

A discussion of the application of critical theory to critical practice must remain incomplete always, because the theories themselves change over time, begin to question themselves and their effectiveness, and generate new, more "relevant" theories. "When a particular theory can no longer encompass new ideas or new works of art, new theories are developed. . . . Each offers a system of useful, but incomplete, organizing constructs which continually lead to new solutions, new problems, and new theories" (Vandergrift, 1990, pp. 1-2). This look at modes of critical theory-in-practice is not meant to be thorough or comprehensive; rather it aims to suggest the illuminating potential of theory in textual criticism.

REFERENCES

Ahlberg, J., & Ahlberg, A. (1986). *The jolly postman, or, Other people's letters*. Boston, MA: Little, Brown.

Anno, M. (1977). *Anno's counting book*. New York: Crowell.

Avi. (1986). Review the reviewers? *School Library Journal, 32*(7), 114-115.

Avi. (1991). *Nothing but the truth: A documentary novel*. New York: Orchard Books.

Babbitt, N. (1987). Fantasy and the classic hero. In B. Harrison & G. Maguire (Comps. & Eds.), *Innocence & experience: Essays & conversations on children's literature* (pp. 148-155). New York: Lothrop, Lee & Shepard.

Campbell, P. J. (1985). *Presenting Robert Cormier*. Boston, MA: Twayne Publishers.

Chambers, A. (1983). *Introducing books to children* (2nd ed.). Boston, MA: Horn Book.

Heins, P. (1970a). Coming to terms with criticism. *Horn Book Magazine, 46*(4), 370-375.

Heins, P. (1970b). Out on a limb with the critics: Some random thoughts on the present state of the criticism of children's literature. *Horn Book Magazine, 46*(3), 264-273.

Hunt, P. (1984-85). Narrative theory and children's literature. *Children's Literature Association Quarterly, 9*(4), 191-194.

Hunt, P. (Ed.). (1990). *Children's literature: The development of criticism*. New York: Routledge.

Hunt, P. (1991). *Criticism, theory, and children's literature*. Oxford, Eng.: Basil Blackwell Ltd.

Kingsbury, M. (1984). Perspectives on criticism. *Horn Book Magazine, 60*(1), 17-23.

Knoepflmacher, U. C. (1992). Introduction. In G. E. Sadler (Ed.), *Teaching children's literature: Issues, pedagogy, resources* (pp. 1-9). New York: Modern Language Association.

Le Guin, U. K. (1968). *A wizard of Earthsea*. Berkeley, CA: Parnassus Press.

Le Guin, U. K. (1979). The child and the shadow. In S. Wood (Ed.), *The language of the night: Essays on fantasy and science fiction* (pp. 59-71). New York: Berkley Pub. Corp.

Lewis, D. (1990, May). The constructedness of texts: Picture books and the metafictive. *Signal*, pp. 131-146.

Mahy, M. (1984). *The changeover: A supernatural romance*. New York: Atheneum.

Moore, O., & MacCann, D. (1990). On canon expansion and the artistry of Joyce Hansen. *Children's Literature Association Quarterly, 15*(1), 33-37.

Moss, A. (Ed.) (1982). Structuralist approaches to children's literature. *Children's Literature Association Quarterly, 7*(3), 33-58.

Moss, G. (1990). Metafiction and the poetics of children's literature. *Children's Literature Association Quarterly, 15*(2), 50-52.

Natov, R. (1990). Mothers and daughters: Jamaica Kincaid's pre-Oedipal narrative. *Children's Literature* (Vol. 18, pp. 1-16). New Haven, CT: Yale University Press.

Paul, L. (1987, September). *Enigma variations: What feminist theory knows about children's literature*. Signal, pp. 186-202.

Phillips, J., & Wojcik-Andrews, I. (1990a). History and the politics of play in T. S. Eliot's 'The burial of the dead' and Arthur Ransome's *Swallows and Amazons*. *The Lion and the Unicorn, 14*(1), 53-69.

Phillips, J., & Wojcik-Andrews, I. (1990b). Notes toward a Marxist critical practice. *Children's Literature* (Vol. 18, pp. 127-130). New Haven, CT: Yale University Press.

Politics and ideology. (1990). *The Lion and the Unicorn, 14*(1).

Roxburgh, S. (1982). *Anno's counting book:* A semiological analysis. *Children's Literature Association Quarterly, 7*(3), 48-52.

Sadler, G. E. (1992). *Teaching children's literature: Issues, pedagogy, resources*. New York: Modern Language Association.

Scieszka, J., & Smith, L. (1992). *The stinky cheese man and other fairly stupid tales*. New York: Viking.

Shavit, Z. (1986). *Poetics of children's literature*. Athens, GA: University of Georgia Press.

Stott, J. C. (1987). The spiralled sequence story curriculum: A structuralist approach to teaching fiction in the elementary grades. *Children's Literature in Education, 18*(3), 148-162.

Thomas, B. (1987). The historical necessity for—and difficulties with—new historical analysis in introductory literature courses. *College English, 49*(5), 509-522.

Thomas, B. (1989). Preserving and keeping order by killing time in *Heart of Darkness*. In R. C. Murfin (Ed.), *Heart of darkness: A case study in contemporary criticism* (pp. 237-258). New York: St. Martin's Press.

Townsend, J. R. (1971). May Hill Arbuthnot honor lecture: Standards of criticism for children's literature. *Top of the News, 27*(4), 373-387.

Vandergrift, K. E. (1990). *Children's literature: Theory, research, and teaching.* Englewood, CO: Libraries Unlimited.

White, M. L. (1976). *Children's literature: Criticism and response.* Columbus, OH: C. E. Merrill Pub. Co.

Woolf, V. (1939). *Reviewing.* London: Hogarth Press.

DOROTHY BRILEY

Editor in Chief
Clarion Books
New York, New York

The Impact of Reviewing on Children's Book Publishing

INTRODUCTION

When Betsy Hearne invited me to speak at this conference, I couldn't quite believe my ears. A chance to review the reviewers. What an opportunity! In preparing to make the most of this golden moment, I've given a lot of thought to reviews, reviewing, and reviewers. In the almost 30 years that I've been involved in publishing children's books, my work has been focused on preparing 25 to 30 books for publication each spring and fall. Each of those 60-odd books a year was begun with the acquisition of an idea or manuscript many months ahead of publication, and was cosseted word by word, line by line, illustration by illustration through the editing and production processes. Each book has had an author (and sometimes an illustrator too) whose hand was held and ego stroked. All that done, seasonal catalog prepared, sales conference held, finished books ordered, and then WHOOSH! in a flash materials were out to reviewers who would decide their fate. All that work involving the expertise of so many—author, editor, copy editor, art director, production staff, sales and marketing departments— willingly offered up to the gods for judgment.

One of the more interesting features of some review journals in which the gods speak is the letters that take exception to opinions expressed in reviews. The letters that interest me most are those from librarians who think the reviewer got it wrong, because in them we have second opinions from professionals who have felt compelled to try to set the record straight. The reviewer, of course, usually gets the last word, but the exchange often causes me to wonder if there is room in the process to make certain that all books get the reviews they deserve. Or does the quality of review that a book receives depend simply on the luck of the draw?

There was a time some years ago when my name and home address were on our mailing list of reviewers so that I could get the books at the same time as the reviewers and know when to start biting my nails. I no longer have this arrangement. That the mails became unreliable is one reason, but also somewhere along the way I stopped holding my breath until the reviews were in. It's not that I stopped caring, but that I find it less wearing to react to reviews in hand than to those anticipated. I liken this bit of personal insight to the epiphany of discovering that there is no point to worrying about the weather. Both reviews and weather are best dealt with when they arrive.

REVIEWS AND THE CHILDREN'S BOOK INDUSTRY

Traditionally, there have been five major influences on the market for children's books. For the record, I list them here alphabetically. ALA *Booklist, The Bulletin of the Center for Children's Books, The Horn Book Magazine, Kirkus Reviews,* and *School Library Journal.* That tradition has its roots in the fact that librarians have always been the major purchasers of children's books. It used to be that the children's book industry was the best-kept secret in the universe. No one knew about us or the books except school and public librarians and the children who borrowed books from those institutions. Apparently, children who did not grow up to be librarians wiped their memories of us completely sometime before leaving high school, never to think of children's books again. We were a tight circle of authors, illustrators, editors, reviewers, and children's librarians.

The circle widened about 15 years ago when a new breed of booksellers began to establish bookstores that sold only children's books. Many of these brave bookselling pioneers were former children's librarians, and they stocked their shelves with their favorite books—the ones they knew from personal experience would appeal to children. Through these stores, the general public became aware that Dr. Seuss was not the only person in the United States writing children's books. For the first time, publishers of hardcover trade books had a sizeable market for some books that did not depend on reviews as a guide to purchase. Booksellers do not use reviews because reviews are not available when publishers' sales representatives call on booksellers. Some booksellers would tell you they wouldn't use reviews if they had them because they know their customers and how to serve them. The result is that some books are already in second printings before reviews begin to appear.

This was the case with *Tuesday* by David Wiesner (1991). The book was published in April, but sales reps had been selling it since mid-December. By March, a month before publication, orders exceeded the first printing of 20,000 copies, and a second printing of the same size was ordered. Then the reviews began arriving. *Publishers Weekly* was first, ending with, "Perhaps because this fantasy never coalesces around a human figure, it is less accessible and less resonant than [Wiesner's] tales that center on a child protagonist" (Roback & Donahue, 1991, p. 73). *Kirkus* gave it a pointer and called it "nifty," but was a little worried about the phase of the moon when it was the pigs' turn to fly (Long, 1991, p. 325). The ABA *Bookseller* declared it a "Pick of the Lists." *School Library Journal* gave it a star and said, "It may not be immortal, but kids will love its lighthearted, meticulously imagined fun-without-a-moral fantasy. *Tuesday* is bound to take off" (Dooley, 1991, p. 86). *The Horn Book* did not review it (silence speaks louder than words) and later ranked it "three" (which means satisfactory) in *The Horn Book Guide to Children's and Young Adult Books* (reviews of books published January through June 1991). *Booklist* didn't give it a star, but its entirely positive review admired it for "allowing for unexpected magic in everyday, modern settings" (Phelan, 1991, p. 1723). *The Bulletin*, after describing the art and story in glowing detail, said, "What saves this book from simply being a gorgeous gallery of paintings is warmth and humor. These frogs are having a lot of fun" (Sutton, 1991, p. 231). The last word was a second thought from *Publishers Weekly*, who apparently liked it better in December than in March, because it was on their list of "Best Books of 1991."

The opinion makers who made the significant impact on sales, needless to say, were the members of the Caldecott committee. We had sold 35,000 copies by the end of 1991 and had ordered a third printing, worrying a little as we did so because it was entirely possible that a good portion of the books sold to bookstores would be shipped back to us in January. That didn't happen. *School Library Journal* got it right. Those frogs took off, and they are still flying.

Tuesday was a sales success prior to the Caldecott Medal. But its sales looked modest when measured against the performance of best-sellers. The reviews were good, but mixed with small cautions. David Wiesner was still in the up-and-coming category. And he wasn't yet a favorite of another category of bookstore that only recently has decided to pay more attention to children's books—the chains.

The selection policies of stores run by Barnes & Noble, Walden, Dalton, and the like are different from those of independent children's-only stores. Up to now, the chains have played it safe and have seldom taken chances on a book by an unknown author. Susan Jeffers' (1991) *Brother Eagle, Sister Sky* was on the *New York Times* and *Publishers Weekly* best-seller lists several weeks before reviewers began to question the book's veracity and authenticity. The number of copies necessary to make the best-seller lists varies from week to week but is always substantial enough to suspect that the chains played a big role in placing *Brother Eagle* there. The reviews critical of the book set off a healthy exchange of opinions that played itself out in the pages of *School Library Journal* for several months and eventually spread to the *New York Times*, *Newsweek,* and *Time Magazine.* The exchange had an important impact. It taught the *New York Times Book Review* to be careful about what it labels nonfiction, but more importantly it heightened awareness of the portrayal of Native Americans in the media in general as well as in children's books. I doubt, though, that it diminished sales. If anything, it may have done just the opposite.

Even before there were retailers buying books without help from reviews, there were always a few books that became popular despite disapproval from professional reviewers. E. B. White's *Stuart Little,* Kay Thompson's *Eloise,* and Robert Cormier's *The Chocolate War* overcame strong, persuasive objections to their use with children years before there were enough booksellers serious enough about children's books to matter much. Helen Bannerman's *Little Black Sambo,* first published in 1906 and well established through the following decades as a "classic," was declared racist by virtually every critic in the field of children's literature during the 1960s. The campaign against its use with children was unrelenting and went on for a number of years. Yet the sales of *Little Black Sambo* never wavered. The book went right along selling 14,000 copies a year throughout the 1960s, 1970s, and 1980s, and continues to do so two years into the 1990s. It has done this without any help from its publishers. For approximately a quarter of a century, *Little Black Sambo* has received no advertising or promotion beyond its listings in *Books in Print* and the publisher's backlist catalog.

It would seem that some books refuse to die, despite all odds. Perhaps this is a healthy sign of a free society, in which there are people who make up their own minds about controversial books regardless of what anyone else has to say. My deep suspicion, though, is that the answer is not as idealistic as all that. I doubt many people beyond the children's book community were ever aware of the controversies. Even though children's books have caught the attention of the general public, the body of professional criticism that has been long associated with them may still be one of the world's best-kept secrets.

Does this mean, then, that reviews don't count—don't have an impact on what gets published, what sells, and what stays in print? I'll admit that there have been a few times in my publishing life when

I wished that were true, but I've lived through those times and probably will again. Most of the time, I happily admit that reviewers are important and essential influences on shaping the books and getting them into children's hands. No publisher of hardcover trade books could survive on its sales to bookstores alone. Out of a list of 30 books, I never expect to see more than 10 titles in bookstores. And out of those 10 titles, several will be what we call "two&watch" orders. This means a bookseller is uncertain and stocks two copies with the intent of ordering more if they get snapped up immediately. "Two&watch" orders are not an expression of vast interest and tend not to be pushed with enthusiasm to customers. Most of them come back to our warehouse as returns.

In my experience, approximately two-thirds of hardcover titles are bought solely by institutions; the majority of sales of the other third, despite trade bookstore distribution, is also institutional. You all know this, but I'll say it anyway: Librarians who buy books for school and public libraries need two to three recommendations from respected review sources to justify their purchases. The news isn't entirely in yet on what the rules will be for classroom teachers when and if they receive funds for books needed to comply with the demand for literature-based curricula. I suspect the rules will be similar to, if not the same as, those for librarians. Even without rules universally in place, the traditional review media already have an impact on classroom purchases. ALA's *Booklinks* is one example of critics already in the field reaching out to teachers and suggesting ways to use the books in curricula contexts. The rapid rise of *Booklinks* subscriptions clearly indicates that it is successfully filling a need in this new marketplace.

Opinions expressed in reviews have influenced how books are put together in a number of ways. Many years ago, I questioned the need for an index in a 32-page nonfiction book with a very short text. I was told that librarians want indexes, period. I was later to learn that illustrations in certain kinds of nonfiction should always be labeled. I learned this from a conversation with the reviewer of a book I hadn't thought needed labels. The practice of attributing the sources of folktales became the rule when reviewers pointed out the need for it. These and many other details, small and large, have added up to a body of publishing do's and don'ts that has raised the standards of creating books for children. The impact of reviews is felt throughout the publishing process, from the editor's desk and even beyond it to the area of subsidiary rights.

Prices that book clubs and paperback reprinters will pay for books, or even whether or not they will buy a book, can be affected by reviews. This is especially true of books by unestablished authors but can also be true of books by some of our best writers. A case in point is Nina Bawden's (1992) new novel, *Humbug*. For various reasons, which I won't go into because they would only be speculation, reprinters responded coolly when *Humbug* was first offered to them. "Too British," said one, though she admitted she hadn't actually read it. So we sat back puzzled for a while. As the reviews came in, gloriously wearing their stars, the reprinters began to call us.

I said I wouldn't speculate on why the reprinters' response to *Humbug* was cool at first, but I've changed my mind. If I'm right, and I think I am, this is something for us all to keep in mind. It is about recognizing the effects that change can have. The moral here is that timing is everything. Paperback editions of Nina Bawden's books have always been published by George Nicholson at Dell. Her books were never shown to other reprinters because George had an option on any Lothrop book that Nina published. I changed jobs three years ago, and *Humbug* is Nina's first new novel with Clarion. Since Dell has no option with Clarion, the book was sent to all the reprinters with the thought that George should have first refusal because of his long-standing interest in the author's work. George left Dell in August, and true to form, the new broom was too busy sweeping to get excited about a book by an author associated with the old regime.

Paperback editors are busy people and have young editors who read and report on submissions. The houses we were submitting to had no previous experience with Nina Bawden, and as much as we'd like to think that a young person working in a publishing house grew up reading the likes of Nina Bawden, there's no guarantee that this is the case. The starred reviews caught the attention of the editors in charge, the book was read, and an auction is taking place the day after tomorrow. Because all aspects of our industry are constantly in a state of change, we must never assume that any writer's reputation is so firmly established that he or she cannot be overlooked.

POSITIVE REVIEWS

Most review journals have some way of indicating the best of the best—the cream of the crop—and, of course, every publisher covets stars. We brag about them, we shout them from the rooftops, we advertise them. We'll even advertise a star from *Booklist* in *School Library Journal* to help counteract the lukewarm review the book received in *School Library Journal*. Give a book a star and the publisher will do its darndest to turn it into a meteor. In looking through the past year's review journals, though, I was struck by how few ads there were for good books, superior books, with good solid reviews. If you judge the scope and diversity of publishers' lists by their advertising, you'd be hard pressed to find some of the best, most important books published—because they didn't get starred reviews and so were not advertised. This phenomenon stems from publishers feeling the squeeze of tight advertising budgets. The state of the economy touches us all. Often after the ads we are obliged to run are paid for, there is not much left for discretionary spending. What reviewers need to realize is that their reviews may be the major support some books receive. If a book is important, but not of star quality, its review becomes all the more instrumental in how well the book sells. Today, more than ever, a great deal of power is in the hands of a very few people.

The journals with the most power are those with the widest distribution. The top five journals I listed alphabetically earlier rank in influence according to the number of subscribers each has. A bad review in one journal *can* cancel out excellent reviews in all the others. It is usually the unique, adventurous book that falls victim to the extreme influence of *one* review over all the others—the times when a new voice is trying to deliver a message in a way not heard before. In tight economic times, without enough money to purchase all the books with starred recommendations, it is understandable that even positive reviews are sometimes being combed for an excuse not to purchase a book.

NEGATIVE REVIEWS

An unfair negative review carries an enormous amount of weight. By an unfair review, I mean one with an agenda other than assessing a book on its merits as literature. Paula Fox (1993) cited a perfect example of an unfair review in her 1988 Zena Sutherland Lecture. She says:

> I hope you will bear with me while I read a few scraps from an evaluation of a book I wrote called *The Moonlight Man.* My intention is to illustrate the murder of language, and therefore of meaning, not to complain about an unsympathetic response. The reviewer writes, "The father . . . is an alcoholic and an interesting, fairly productive person . . . the daughter acts as a facilitator for his alcoholism which is not a healthy role model for students who may face this problem. The book is about her separation from her parents as individuals, but it closes with her father abandoning her. The task of final separation from parents does not belong to junior high students and I do not think this age needs to face parental abandonment. Furthermore, if a child is dealing with an alcoholic parent, this book does not give acceptable guidance to work on that problem." (p. 116)

Paula Fox (1993) then goes on to expand on that review with these words:

> I believe this report to contain a basic perversion of what literature and stories are concerned with—the condition of being human. It is written in the jargon of social science. The writer does not like the book and is unable to say so. Instead, she evokes a contemporary vision of virtue and

sin: productivity and unproductivity. The father should be the daughter's client—or patient. The story is not acceptable because it does not give "guidance."

What I am concerned with here is the deadening of language, an extreme form of alienation expressed in words that have no resonance, and absolutely no inner reference to living people. "This age does not need to face parental abandonment," the reviewer writes. Leaving aside the question of whether or not abandonment is involved, what on earth is "this age?" Who need not face what? Which boys? Which girls? What human beings? (pp. 116-117)

The perversion of what literature and stories are concerned with, which Paula has so ably put forth, is not uncommon. Even reviewers who do not distance themselves with social science jargon too many times get caught up with wanting writers to give them stories that will mold the character of the reader into whatever is thought to be the "right" shape. It is admirable to want to give children guidance on ways to protect themselves when they are caught up in unfortunate circumstances. But storytelling concerns itself with the way people actually behave, not how they *should* behave or even how they *would* behave if they had the benefit of the best guidance society can provide. In fact, the very story that Paula Fox wrote could lead a child reader living in a similar circumstance to recognize his or her situation— recognition being the key step toward seeking help.

Another example of well-meant but wrong-headed reviewing was of Russell Freedman's (1992) *An Indian Winter.* After giving a fine, succinct description of the book's content, the reviewer added this zinger at the end: "The book is generously . . . illustrated, chiefly with works by Bodmer, whose watercolors of individuals are direct and immediate. However, engravings later produced in Europe seem stereotyped. . . . Readers of Freedman's other titles on Native American topics will find much of interest here, though some may question the reliability of two European dilettantes concerning a culture they visited only briefly" (Roback & Donahue, 1992, p. 58). Where did these comments come from? Were they prompted by the book that Russell Freedman wrote? Or is this reviewer, to quote Arthur M. Schlesinger, Jr. (1992), one of those "self styled 'multiculturalists' [who] are very often ethnocentric separatists who see little in the Western heritage beyond Western crimes" (p. 123)? In our zeal to recognize and give fair representation to American cultural diversity, are we now promoting the idea that, in Schlesinger's words again, "The Western tradition . . . is inherently racist, sexist, 'classist', hegemonic; irredeemably repressive, irredeemably oppressive" (p. 123)?

Consider this, from a review of Andersen's *The Nightingale*, retold by Michael Bedard (1991) with illustrations by Regolo Ricci: "The pictures are detailed, delicate watercolors in a westernized Chinese style. Costumes and settings are extravagant: conventional imperial clutter and color abound (and the jacket notes attest to the authenticity of some of the motifs). All of the faces, alas, appear to be caricatures, wizened and jaundiced, mottled and sickly, with exaggeratedly 'oriental' eyes. These unappealing portraits . . . make the book a poor competitor against the edition illustrated by Lisbeth Zwerger" (Dooley, 1992, p. 85).

Whether one agrees that Ricci's illustrations do not compete well with Zwerger's (she is also a Westerner, and so was Hans Christian Andersen, by the way) is not the point. Why is "westernized" now a negative adjective? What is being said? Is Ricci being accused of "westernizing" Chinese style? If so, has he? What are "exaggeratedly 'oriental' eyes?" While it is true that the Emperor is portrayed as "wizened and jaundiced, mottled and sickly," he does spend much of the book on his deathbed. The point is whether or not "political correctness" is rearing its head in children's book reviewing. If so, we may be in danger of contributing to the unfortunate trend toward a divisive culture, which is very different from accepting and celebrating cultural diversity.

PROBLEMATIC REVIEWS

Good reviews can sometimes be as problematic as unfair reviews, particularly in times when book selectors are trying to winnow down the numbers of titles to choose from for economic reasons. An example of positive reviews that recommend a book for purchase and use with children, but that unwittingly gave book selectors ammunition to reject it, is from this spring's reviews of *Long Spikes* by Jim Arnosky (1992). One review reads, "*National Geographic* specials will have prepared animal lovers for the kind of blunt, tooth-and-claw hunting action here, and readers who are not generally absorbed by wildlife lore will appreciate the story's brisk pace." However, the review also says, "Although the text once or twice slips into slightly anthropomorphic terms (Long Spikes is once 'entranced' by mayflies and again 'enthralled' by his reflection), the story is generally as clear-headed as it is clearly written" (Hearne, 1992, p. 198). Another reviewer in another journal says that "Arnosky offers a story brimming with reality . . . a true glimpse into the natural world, a world that is getting smaller all the time," but also says, "There are only the barest hints of anthropomorphism, but these are made plausible by the details that could only come from careful observation" (Oliver, 1992, p. 111).

Now, anthropomorphism is a subject I have long wanted to discuss with opinion makers in the children's literature field. I first became interested in how children's book reviewers treat this subject many years ago on reading a review of one of Hope Ryden's children's books, in which the reviewer chastised Ryden severely for committing anthropomorphism. I was familiar with Ryden's books for adults, particularly her then recently published *God's Dog* (Ryden, 1975), and admired her ability to report her observations in the field without prejudice—scientific or otherwise. Her work was a refreshing antidote to the pronouncements of animal behaviorists who drew their conclusions from studies of animals in captivity. I found her observations exciting and was delighted that she was willing to share them with children, but here was a reviewer who thought children should be protected from them.

I do not wish to challenge the universally held notion that anthropomorphism in natural history books for children is a literary crime, but I would like to challenge what is considered to be anthropomorphic. As for Jim Arnosky's book, to my knowledge the states of mind implied by the words "entranced" and "enthralled" are not restricted to human beings. If anthropomorphism is a crime, shouldn't anthropocentrism be a crime of equal measure? Are we so far removed from the natural world that we do not recognize how much we have in common with other animals with whom we share this world that is "getting smaller all the time?" In the words of the second reviewer, the behaviors Jim Arnosky described were "made plausible by the details that could only come from careful observation" (Oliver, 1992, p. 111).

Now for the effect of the Arnosky reviews: Last week I received two more reviews of *Long Spikes*. These are from an independent school district in Texas. Both reviewers indicate on the forms sent to us that they have seen the reviews I just read. The first review rates the book Not Recommended, and says: "Long Spikes, a deer who is orphaned as a yearling when his mother is killed, grows to maturity. The animal is given human feelings making it too unrealistic." Period. Apparently, this media center must have two opinions to kill a book; the second reviewer writes, "Long Spikes and his sister are orphaned as yearlings. Their challenges to survival are chronicled from the animals' point of view. This story is really packed with information on the life cycle and behavioral traits of the white-tailed deer. Because it is brief and clearly presented, the book could be used in research." At this point, I thought there was a glimmer of hope for Long Spikes, but the reviewer goes on, "There is no index, however. One would have to be highly motivated for information or be a very serious animal lover because the story is not sufficient to keep the average middle schooler reading" (Round Rock Independent School District, Austin, Texas). Here's something else: Has anyone ever seen an *average* middle schooler? What does an average child look like? There are a lot of books that aren't bought in his name. I've never seen a review that said, "average children will love this." But back to anthropomorphism. My point is only to demonstrate the power the major reviews have. My personal quibble over what anthropomorphism is and isn't is another discussion. I just want everyone to know that the A-word is a guaranteed deterrent to sales, no matter how it is used in a review.

DOCUMENTATION IN NONFICTION

Most children's book editors were brought up on Walter de la Mare's words, "Only the very best is good enough for children," and work diligently to apply this philosophy to all the books they publish. It came as a great surprise to discover in an article that appeared in the May 1991 issue of *School Library Journal* (Broadway & Howland, 1991) that publishers and writers of nonfiction, science books in particular, are viewed with almost paranoid suspicion. The authors of the article reported the results of a survey they had made of nonfiction writers, which revealed that few were specialists in subjects they write about, and concluded that "Librarians, library media specialists, and selectors of informational books for children . . . must insist that publishers require authors to demonstrate their authority in the subject areas in which they write." "Certainly," they go on to say, "education, experience, and interest in a topic are three manifestations of authority. Well-documented research is another barometer of authority that is needed in children's books" (p. 38).

There is much that I could say about the method and scope of the survey that Broadway and Howland conducted, as well as their apparent lack of understanding of how to produce good nonfiction children's books. However, it is their last sentence that is pertinent to this discussion. To repeat, "Well-documented research is another barometer of authority that is needed in children's books." No responsible publisher or writer would argue with this point, but why is it phrased to suggest that children's books in general are remiss in this respect? Attribution of quotations and paraphrasings within the text, plus a bibliography of sources, has been common practice for many years. Have the rules been changed? Must documentation be in a certain form in order to be acceptable? The reviews of the past two years have been very confusing about this. Books with exactly the same form of documentation pass muster with some reviewers and not with others— sometimes within the pages of the same journal. It is important to get to the bottom of this for two reasons: Reviews are beginning to appear that spend almost as much space reviewing the documentation as is given to the book, and a negative review of the bibliography or the words "No documentation" can be a deciding factor when the book is considered for purchase. This is unfair to writers who have made an effort to identify their sources.

A clear statement on what constitutes acceptable documentation that all reviewers subscribe to would be very useful. It's possible that many writers of informational books would be willing and able to comply with whatever form the opinion makers dictate. Those writers not willing to comply would at least know what they are up against. This entire matter is between writers and their audience. Publishers have no stake in this one way or the other, except when confusion results in loss of book sales.

In the event editors of the review journals take me seriously and try to formulate such a statement, I feel obligated to offer a few warnings. First, many highly respected writers of nonfiction books view their bibliographies and/or notes as further communication with their child readers, and it will come as a great shock to them that reviewers are looking at these sections to determine whether or not authors have done their homework. Two, footnotes referenced to superscripts within the text would not be a welcome suggestion to those writers who justifiably take great pride in having perfected the craft of writing responsibly and informatively without having to resort to the conventions of academia. Three, the argument that writers should at the very least conform to the conventions expected of students when writing term papers could possibly lead to serious bloodshed. The more controlled writers would simply end all discussion with the statement, "I don't do term papers," but others would probably attack with whatever weapon is handy. I don't have a solution to this problem, but I do have a wish. I wish there were more stress on how important it is to encourage children to read nonfiction.

CONCLUSION

The answer to the question I posed at the beginning, "Is there room in the process to make certain that all books get the reviews they deserve?" is, of course, no. This is no more possible than the expectation that all books be properly written, edited, and published. The writers, illustrators, publishers, reviewers, librarians, and booksellers who make up the children's book community are after all imperfect humans. Though difficult economic times may exacerbate our differences, the miracle of it is that we are all focused on accomplishing the same goal— placing good books into the hands of children. I don't know of any other group that undergoes as much constant self-examination in the name of doing our individual jobs better than the children's book community. This Allerton Institute is of course a prime example of that ongoing process. Though these remarks have been largely critical, they are meant to be constructive, and I now willingly offer them up to the gods for review. Thank you for this golden moment.

REFERENCES

Arnosky, J. (1992). *Long Spikes: A story*. New York: Clarion Books.

Bawden, N. (1992). *Humbug*. New York: Clarion Books.

Bedard, M. (1991). *The nightingale*. Illustrated by R. Ricci. New York: Clarion Books.

Broadway, M. D., & Howland, M. (1991). Science books for young people: Who writes them? *School Library Journal, 37*(5), 35-38.

Dooley, P. (1991). Review of *Tuesday* by D. Wiesner. *School Library Journal, 37*(5), 86.

Dooley, P. (1992). Review of Hans Christian Andersen's *The nightingale*, retold by M. Bedard. *School Library Journal, 38*(5), 85.

Fox, P. (1993). Unquestioned answers. In B. Hearne (Ed.), *The Zena Sutherland lectures 1983-1992*. New York: Clarion Books.

Freedman, R. (1992). *An Indian winter*. Illustrated by K. Bodmer. New York: Holiday House.

Hearne, B. (1992). Review of *Long Spikes* by J. Arnosky. *Bulletin of the Center for Children's Books, 45*(8), 198.

Jeffers, S. (1991). *Brother Eagle, Sister Sky: A message from Chief Seattle*. Illustrated by S. Jeffers. New York: Dial.

Long, J. R. (Ed.). (1991). Review of *Tuesday* by D. Wiesner. *Kirkus Children's and Young-Adult Edition, 59*(5), 325 (C-63).

Oliver, S. (1992). Review of *Long Spikes* by J. Arnosky. *School Library Journal, 38*(5), 111.

Phelan, C. (1991). Review of *Tuesday* by D. Wiesner. *Booklist, 87*(17), 1723.

Roback, D., & Donahue, R. (Eds.). (1991, Mar. 1). Review of *Tuesday* by D. Wiesner. *Publishers Weekly*, p. 73.

Roback, D., & Donahue, R. (Eds.). (1992, May 4). Review of *An Indian winter* by R. Freedman. *Publishers Weekly*, p. 58.

Ryden, H. (1975). *God's dog*. New York: Coward, McCann & Geoghegan.

Schlesinger, A. M., Jr. (1992). *The disuniting of America*. New York: W. W. Norton.

Sutton, R. (1991). Review of *Tuesday* by D. Wiesner. *Bulletin of the Center for Children's Books, 44*(9), 231.

Wiesner, D. (1991). *Tuesday*. New York: Clarion Books.

GRACIELA ITALIANO

Lecturer
Department of Ethnic and Women's Studies
California Polytechnic University
Pomona, California

Reading Latin America: Issues in the Evaluation of Latino Children's Books in Spanish and English

DEFINITIONS

The topic that I was asked to discuss here this morning is very important—to you, obviously, because you're including it in your conference; and to me, because I've spent over 20 years trying to make some sense of how the bridging between cultures can be done via children's literature. Before I even begin, let me talk about the basics— the power of naming. Why do we say Latino and not Hispanic? Why do we say Chicano and not Latino or Hispanic or Latin American? I know this is confusing, but there may be experiences in your own life where you have been in touch with the same phenomenon. We are talking about the power of self-naming. Naming is very important because it identifies, it creates, a certain aspect of the personality. Different ethnic groups in this country and all over the world are in the process of empowering themselves, and naming, self-naming, is part of that process.

For the purpose of this presentation, I will use the word *Latino*, meaning anybody of Latin American descent, born either there or here. There's another definition I need to work with, and that is the word *Chicano*. The term *Chicano* was taken, in the process of renaming, by a certain part of the population of Hispanics in this country during the 1960s civil rights movement. The term *Chicano* really refers to a political philosophy of re-empowerment, of digging for roots and

119

looking into history and re-creating myths, such as those of Aztlan. Persons who have designated themselves *Chicanos* say, "We've been here a long, long time, we're not newcomers, we're not invaders, we're not illegals, and yes, we are Chicanos." Many times, I use the terms *Latino* and *Chicano* interchangeably. Often, people ask me if I consider myself a Chicana, and I have come to understand that because I've spent over 20 years in this country, even though I was born and raised in Uruguay, I feel a very strong kinship to the political philosophy that the Chicano movement expresses. So, I will claim to be a Chicana, though for today, I will use the more inclusive term *Latino*.

In any language, *literature* must be defined before we can proceed with a discussion of its criticism. Of course, literature can be defined in many ways, but I would like to use Rebecca Lukens' (1990) definition of literature as "reading that, by means of imaginative and artistic qualities, provides pleasure and understanding" (p. 5). Then we get into what is the subject of criticism. Again, Lukens puts it in very simple terms: "it is the function of the writer to make sense out of life, but the function of the critic is to evaluate the writer's efforts to make sense out of life" (p. 4). That's why we're here, trying to evaluate the writer's efforts to make sense out of life. And, of course, this definition fits my topic very well because, while life is understood by all of us in human terms all over the world, life is manifested culturally in many different ways. That's where our problems in evaluating children's books on Latino issues, whether in Spanish or English, come from; even though we share a humanity, many times we don't share the way humanity is manifested.

CULTURE AND LANGUAGE

I find two main areas of difficulty: One is lack of familiarity with the culture a book is portraying, and in the case of books in Spanish, ignorance of the language. If the book is written in Spanish and you don't speak Spanish, we've got a problem.

Many books, fortunately, are now being published bilingually, with a text in English and Spanish, and I could cite all kinds of educational research on both sides of the argument as to whether bilingual books are good or bad. Provided they are well laid out and designed, and that they're not confusing—as you turn the page (if you're following the Spanish) you're not groping for where the Spanish text is—bilingual books work very well for children and adults who want to share them with children.

Again, there's the issue of language. Language and culture cannot be separated. We separate them in order to make it easier to look at these constructs in a linear form, but they cannot be separated. If you think for a moment, our language is us. Our language is our culture and our culture is our language. The way we speak represents us as much as does the way we look. Groups may share many other elements besides language, but language is a powerful way for people to feel ethnic kinship.

I use, in my multicultural classes, a book by James Banks (1991), who defines ethnic groups as groups whose members share a unique social and cultural heritage, passed on from one generation to the next. Ethnic groups are frequently identified by distinctive patterns of family life—recreation, religion, and other customs—that differentiate them from others. Above all else, members of such groups feel a consciousness of kind, an interdependence of fate, with those who share the same ethnic tradition. An individual is ethnic to the extent that he or she shares the language, values, behavioral patterns, cultural traits, and identification with a specific ethnic group. Many individuals have multiple ethnic group attachments.

According to Banks (1991), the three major groups of Latinos in the United States are Mexican-Americans, Puerto Ricans, and Cuban-Americans. In addition, a substantial number of immigrants from Central and South America have entered the United States since 1970, and I could spend a whole hour just discussing why that happened. I belong to this last group, a South American who entered after the 1970s because our continent was in enormous political upheaval, and many of us had to leave for the sake of our own lives.

The Latino population is growing about five times faster than the rest of the U.S. population, and it is misleading to conceptualize these diverse groups of immigrants as one people; they have wide cultural, racial, and ethnic differences. I want to stop here for a minute and qualify this. I say we are different, we are diverse, and it is misleading to bunch us all together, particularly as the term Hispanic tends to do. Yet we do have a culture in common because we shared a conquest that was quite strong; Spanish was superimposed on many, many rich Indian languages that were there. As you know, conquest standardizes. So we do have a culture in common.

The beauty about the Latin American continent and Latinos who have been in this country even for generations, as in the case of New Mexico, is that we hold on to what was there before, in some places more than others. That's what creates the problem: There was richness of culture and language to begin with; then there was the super-imposition of the culture and language of the Spaniards or the Europeans (in the case of Brazil, it was mostly Portuguese); and then there's a syncretism that happens on the American continent, which isn't over—we're still in the midst of this.

We understand, or are beginning to understand, that we are *mestizos,* we are mixed. We have three major strands present in all of our cultures: the indigenous, the European, and the African. You will find many Latin Americans not wanting to acknowledge that, and I do believe it is a question of color—the darker is the more difficult to accept.

Not all countries readily accept their indigenous backgrounds and the presence of indigenous peoples there. Don't forget that when we talk about a national culture, we're really talking about the dominant class culture, which for the most part in Latin America still remains a very small percentage—4% to 8% of the population, mostly claiming European backgrounds, in control of 90% of the resources, and all of the media, and supposedly the national culture. So we have a lot of variables here.

Our language changes, even though we understand each other. (This is a great misconception that people have here, that we speak such different Spanish that we don't understand each other. We do—if we want to. That's the trick.) Sometimes you find, when there is a group of Latin Americans together and particularly when there is a non-Latin American involved, that we like to play this game: "That's not the right way to say that." "No, we don't say it that way; that's wrong." Well, there are standard rules for the language, and Spanish is much more standardized than English, in spelling and grammar. As in any language, however, the local color and variation of the vocabulary is not right or wrong. So you must guard against Latin Americans ego-tripping with, "This is the correct way to say it." There are many stories and legends about why certain countries claim the most proper Spanish.

When I refer to the Latino culture, you will understand that as we get closer to each other, and as we have more children's books coming from the Latino culture, we will have to become much more cognizant of all these variations. However, speaking generally about a Latino culture makes sense because we need to be roughly tuned to bridge non-Latinos to Latinos.

CHILDREN'S BOOKS IN SPANISH AND ENGLISH

The avoidance of stereotyped images of characters, plot, setting, theme, point of view, and style in text and illustrations is paramount if children of all ethnicities are to be presented with literature that makes sense out of life rather than distorts and confuses it. Characters are revealed in different ways to varying degrees of complexity according to the genre of the story and to the level of importance within the story. Whatever the role of a particular character within the story, consistency of personality and actions is always required. Here, I would like to turn to specific books to develop my argument because I don't want to continue speaking in the abstract. I want to begin with a book called *El Sombrero de Tio Nacho/Uncle Nacho's Hat* (Rohmer, 1989). In this book, published by Children's Book Press, Uncle Nacho's dilemma and actions are consistent with the cultural context of many countries in Latin America. Basically, his dilemma is that he has this old hat that he practically swears at every morning because it is of no use any more, and on one of their morning visits his niece comes and gives him a new hat. Then the whole book is about how he cannot get rid of his old hat because he's too attached to it. This is consistent with Latin American or Latino values because in most of our culture, and in most of our social classes, it is not conceivable to throw things away because there is always someone else who might need them. And this includes throwing away values!

To a person familiar with Latin American culture, the actions in this book make sense; they are familiar. They depict an aspect of the culture that *feels* authentic. I realize that's not a very scientific way of defining it, of helping you, but that is the truth. You pick up a book, and if you are familiar with this culture, you say, yes, this resonates. And if it doesn't, then you start looking for why it doesn't. But the initial reaction is a gut-level feeling that this is going in the right direction.

Uncle Nacho gets up in the morning and says "good morning" to his parrot, to his monkey, to his dog, to his cat. I grew up seeing my grandmother doing the same thing, seeing my mother do the same thing. A sentence on the first page, "Uncle Nacho lit the fire," is very important in defining the setting. We know he is in rural Latin America. I didn't grow up with a wood stove inside the house, but in summers when I went to visit my mother's family in the interior of the country, that's how they did it. They had charcoal or wood, and before you had morning coffee, you had to light the fire. It makes sense, in rural Latin America, to have this happening today. You may have people who say that's not the *only* thing that happens in Latin America. True, we have urban centers, enormous cities, very modern and technified in many ways, but one thing doesn't exclude the other.

Then Ambrosia, his niece, comes in: "She always stopped in for a little visit on her way to school." That's the way it happens. Family members live near each other, and they visit each other several times during a day, to check on each other. I used to go to piano lessons twice a week, and my two grandmothers lived on the way from my house to my piano lesson so they knew which days I had piano lessons, and they were waiting for me with little snacks, and they knew what time I came and what time I left. There is a whole network of extended family that works in this manner. The person who was writing this book knows. It's not an outsider's view.

By "outsider" I don't necessarily mean somebody who was not born in the culture. It may be somebody from within the culture who has chosen to look at it as an outsider, or it may be somebody who was not born within the culture who has taken the time and energy and sincerity to explore within the culture, to look as an insider. I do not think that one has to be of a particular ethnic group to write a book about that group; I do think one has to have integrity in the task one has undertaken and to be, or become, familiar with the culture so that the book does not portray stereotypes of any kind.

The setting in *Uncle Nacho's Hat,* a tropical island somewhere in Latin America, is practically never described; yet the illustrator, Veg Reisberg, has done an excellent job of developing a sense of place. Since I travel in Latin America, I can identify this as Puerto Rico, Nicaragua, some place in Central America. South America might look like this in the summer, but even so, our color schemes are a bit different because the pampas are different from the equatorial countries. Somebody who has traveled can pick up the difference right away.

The illustrator has a lot to do with how all these elements, particularly setting and tone, are developed. The illustrator has a wonderful opportunity to enrich a story, to fill it with detail without detracting from it, if he or she integrates the illustrations with the text.

The bilingual design of the text—English on the top and Spanish on the bottom, with a little hat in front of each paragraph of each different language—is a little too crowded for my taste, but I've read this book out loud many times, and it works. I don't have to be going all over the place looking for the text.

One word of caution about the linguistic process: This particular tale was collected by Harriet Rohmer in Latin America, in Nicaragua. Of course, it was originally told in Spanish, but her text is originally in English. So there's already been a translation, and then someone else, Rosalma Zubizaretta [and Alma Ada] took the English text and translated it into Spanish. You can see the many stages this goes through. I personally find that by the time we get to the Spanish text here, it's correct but has lost some of its color.

There's a conscious attempt on the part of many of us who translate and edit and review the Spanish text to go for safely neutral language. When I get in my assertive mood, I say, "Show me somebody who speaks that language! In what country do they speak this neutral Spanish? Whose national anthem is sung in this neutral Spanish? Whose folk songs are sung in this neutral Spanish?"

Living in New York for 10 years, I participated in plays with all kinds of Latin Americans, and we always had weeks before we started rehearsing trying to figure out whose Spanish we were going to use, what accent, how we were going to pronounce the S's. It's really complicated, and at the same time, we make it more complicated than it is.

El Sombrero de Tio Nacho is a story from Nicaragua; I wouldn't see anything wrong if this text had some local color or vocabulary from Nicaragua that could have been explained at the back of the book or somewhere in notes, in a proper way. This neutrality results from trying to bridge to another culture whose native language is not Spanish. We are always concerned that if we put words in there that are a little bit off the mainstream path, people will say, "Well, you see these people don't understand each other; they all speak different kinds of Spanish. How are we supposed to buy it?"

The second book I'd like to share with you is called *My Aunt Otilia's Spirits/Los Espiritus de Mi Tia Otilia* (Garcia, 1987). It's also from Children's Book Press, and in this particular case, the author is Richard Garcia, and he is of Mexican descent—Mexican mother and Puerto Rican father. He was familiar with the Mexican side of his family but wanted to explore the Puerto Rican and came up with this story about La Tia Otilia, who is actually from Puerto Rico. The story is about how she comes to visit a boy and his family in San Francisco.

Garcia, in a very humorous way, explains that Tia Otilia was accompanied by bed shakings and wall knockings wherever she went. Now, in every Latin American family, and maybe in some of yours too, there is always an aunt, an uncle, a grandfather, a grandmother who is accompanied by late bed shakings and strange noises wherever they go. I'm talking about that one person in the family who is a bit strange. The difference may be that in Latin American culture we find them colorful and accept them in a way that not all cultures do.

Richard Garcia is using childhood memories of the strange one coming to visit: "Because there was little room in our house, Aunt Otilia used to share my bed." I read that and, immediately, the feeling of authenticity comes back to me. This guy knows what he is talking about. And it's not always because there's no room in the house. I lived in a very big house, and I slept with my grandmother until I was six years old. It was considered appropriate; there was closeness; and it's true—she taught me all kinds of things in bed at night, from praying, to discussing the day's events, to dealing with my mother and my father. There was bonding between my grandmother and me because we were sharing a bed. Later on, we shared a room, and then she remarried and I had to mourn her loss for I don't know how long. This is very common. This rings true.

The extended family encourages children and adults to share things, not only beds and rooms, but time together, and I see that present in

Garcia's book. Because Aunt Otilia did not live with them, this boy is particularly afraid of what happens when he goes to sleep because there are rapping sounds and other goings-on. He decides he's going to put chewing gum in his ears, a very childlike thing to do, in order to stay awake, to see where these sounds are coming from. She tells him to go to sleep, but he doesn't. He stays awake, and soon enough the bed rattles, and there's all this noise, and he sees her bones leaving her body, going through the window and out into the night. He's terrified, absolutely terrified, and in his shaking with fear, he stumbles out of bed, and in the process, her body falls all over the floor.

He hurries to put it back together on the bed, but he is so afraid that he puts the arms where the legs should be and the head where the feet should be, and at that point, she comes back, or her bones come back, and she says, "Oh, you bad boy. Put my pieces back right," and her bones are floating outside the window and he is too frightened to move. Of course, the next morning, the sun comes up and her bones fade away, her voice gets farther away, her pieces fade away, her suitcases fade away, and she is gone like a bad dream.

The ending does not explain the events because the events do not need explanation. They are part of what we call magical reality. Latin American literary production in this century has been prolific, and I attribute this to the fact that we are a continent with so many conflicts. We are forced to deal with them whether we want to or not, and writing is certainly one way to deal with conflicts.

We have produced some of the most interesting literature written anywhere in the world during the 20th century. Some of it is starting to be translated, and it is called magical realism; in Spanish we call it *realismo mágico*. It has provided a way for us to understand our own reality, which borders constantly on the magical in the sense that our delineations between the real world and the spirit world are not as clear-cut as in other cultures. We live with healers, we live with people who rap on the bed and who have bad dreams, and we pay attention to them and tell each other our dreams and try to explain life events by our dreams. We weave dreams into our own clothing.

We also live with a lot of violence. In countries where revolution after revolution is constantly taking place, you are constantly losing people. In order not to go crazy, you stay connected to those who have died, to those who have gone away to other countries to survive or to learn another language or to travel. It is an incredible syncretism of many cultures that allows magical realism to make sense—within the culture and as a product of the culture—when you start reading the work of authors such as Garcia Marquez in *One Hundred Years of Solitude,* or Octavio Paz, who won the Nobel Prize last year for *The Labyrinth of Solitude.* The Nobel Peace Prize was just given to

Rigoberta Menchu, a Guatemalan Indian whose need to communicate her people's ordeal was such that she wrote an incredible book, via a ghostwriter, when she barely had learned to speak Spanish. The person who did the actual writing, after many sessions of interviewing Rigoberta Menchu, stayed very true to Menchu's linguistic use of Spanish, which of course is imbued with her Indian language.

When you start reading these books—and I hope you do because there's no better way to evaluate Latino children's books than to become familiar with Latino culture—your immediate reaction, in many cases, will be, "Oh, how imaginative!" What I want to convey to you right now is that these authors are only recording reality in a memorable way. They use a lot of their own skills, but our Latin American reality is very much as these books present it. The writers are not imagining a new, fantastic reality but are drawing from their own experiences and their own families, as well as from a rich oral tradition full of magic folklore. This is why I feel *Los Espiritus de Mi Tia Otilia* is important to share with children. After I read aloud a couple of books dealing with this magical aspect of our reality, I can't tell you the kinds of stories that flow in the room. We go into storytelling and writing with both children and adults.

The review editors' panel discussion addressed how we sometimes prop up a book that we may not be so crazy about in certain aspects because the subject is so much in demand. I am not particularly crazy about the illustration in *Los Espiritus,* to be honest with you, but because of the thematic elements I have just considered, sometimes I let go of my critical analysis of certain aspects of a book. I'm not justifying, or saying that's the way to do it, but for me it's a reality. There are so few of these books that I feel are authentic, that I often overlook flaws. I hope, if I have a chance to talk with the author or the illustrator or the editor, to make my point, but I nurture the books because they need nurturing.

I want to examine a different kind of book that picks up the magical element very well. This is the book *Abuela* by Arthur Dorros (1991), illustrated by Elisa Kleven. Many more of you have seen *Abuela* than have seen *Uncle Nacho* or *Aunt Otilia,* and I'll tell you why. Because it's in English. It was also reviewed. It has been more of a mainstream book from the beginning. I happened to meet the editor of this book, and if we have time I'll tell you some of the stories of her ordeal with finding an illustrator for *Abuela.*

What Dorros has done so masterfully here is to intertwine two languages. The book is in English, but it has sentences like "Abuela is my grandma. She is my mother's mother. *Abuela* means 'grandma' in Spanish. Abuela speaks mostly Spanish because that's what people spoke where she grew up. . . . *'El parque es lindo,'* says Abuela. I know what she means. I think the park is beautiful t(·)." It flows. He is not translating literally from English to Spanish but is taking you along, as he tells you the story, in two languages. That's how most of us who are bilingual think, and speak, when we are among other bilinguals. This requires a certain familiarity with both languages and therefore both cultures. He's done it so that people who are not bilingual can appreciate this. That is what I find so unique about the book.

We always say, if you're going to speak English, speak English; if you're going to speak Spanish, speak Spanish. But it's not so when you're really interested in communicating with someone else who you know is also bilingual and has lived in this country. There are words in English that, in order to explain them in Spanish, you have to go through a 10-minute explanation. So you're speaking in Spanish and boom—here comes a concept in English or vice versa. Speaking bilingually implies intimacy, cultural intimacy, ethnic intimacy. A shared experience of life. And I think this book captures that very well. The magical element? The whole adventure is about flying. You find that flying is a recurring theme in magical realism, symbolizing the flight of the spirit in imagination. Many names come to me: Isabel Allende, from Chile, has just published a trilogy, in which several characters float around several times. *The House of the Spirits* is the first book. The second one is *De Amor y de Sombra/Of Love and Shadows*. The third one is *Eva Luna*. In *One Hundred Years of Solitude*, Rosaura Buendía one day is taking a bath and just floats into outer space and we never hear of that character again; everybody just assumes she has floated away forever.

In Dorros' book, Abuela and the narrator fly all over New York City and have the most wonderful adventures as they speak in both languages. "'Come, Abuela,' I'd say. '*Si, quiero volar,*' Abuela would reply as she leaped into the sky with her skirt flapping in the wind."

Of course we have the flying theme in English-speaking traditions, too, and this is where the story of the editor comes in. Donna Brooks, at Dutton, looked more than two years for somebody who was Latino to illustrate this book. Elisa Kleven, who is not Latino, nevertheless did an excellent job of illustrating *Abuela*. She has a folk art style that fits the story very well, as do the bright colors. Many of these books, including *Uncle Nacho* and *Aunt Otilia*, have bright colors. You are not going to find many pastels in Latin American culture. The children are used to bright colors; our houses are decorated with them. If you've been even as close as Mexico, you immediately know there's a different perception of color in our culture. It comes from an Indian tradition of colors that reflect the natural world of brilliant flowers and bird feathers. It also comes from the African presence in Latin America.

Kleven has also captured the feeling of shared intimacy between this grandmother and grandchild. In several places, the text refers to an extended family: As Abuela and the narrator fly by, they notice Tio Daniel working in the docks; then they come down and visit Tio Pablo and Tia Elisa's little store somewhere.

At a conference that I organized recently, Dorros spoke on how the multicultural experience relates to the universal experience. He has traveled extensively through Latin America, backpacking; we had a lot of stories to share, he and I, of backpacking through the Andes, Bolivia, and Peru on trucks with Indians who did not speak Spanish, of how we eventually were taken in and able to spend time with them. His wife is from Colombia, and Spanish is spoken in the house, along with English. In other words, he is not Latin American. Big deal. He understands. And he has portrayed us in a very authentic way.

The last book I want to discuss is one with which I had some trouble. *Diego* is illustrated by Jeannette Winter, written by Jonah Winter (1992), and published by Knopf. Let me start with the reason I had trouble. I loved the book and felt its authenticity immediately. Yet I had trouble, as a critic, with the lack of plot, antagonism, conflict. I always have a committee in my head, and they fight very hard. My training in children's literature came from the American side of my schooling, and I taught children's literature before I ever got into trying to look at children's literature in Spanish. Some of the elements are very difficult to bridge.

In this particular case, I kept thinking, well, where is the plot children will expect? I finally said that I have to go with my positive response; if I'm going to talk about a feeling, then I just have to be able to follow my own advice, and I included *Diego* in this presentation because it's a very well-tuned book. Even though neither author nor illustrator is Latino, the tone of Jeanette Winter's illustrations are so loving to the Mexican culture that you can't help feeling it immediately in the first picture. She has done the illustrations as if they are framed paintings that you are viewing in an exhibit. A magical element is introduced immediately. When the Mexican muralist Diego Rivera is born, his twin brother dies, and the doctor recommends that the parents get a nurse. They get *una curandera*, an Indian healer, and send Diego to her little hut in the mountains. In one illustration, you see the curandera on a burro, going up a hill covered with maguey, which is the cacti from which tequila is made. She takes little Diego to her hut in the mountains. "Inside there were magical things. There was an altar with candles and little dolls. There were all sorts of herbs and dried fruits. Antonia used these in her healing."

Let me read a little bit of the Spanish because I feel this book, even though it doesn't use local vocabulary, is a good example of poetic language in Spanish. "Adentro había cosas mágicas. Había un altar con velas y muñecas pequeñas. Había todo tipo de hierbas y frutas secas. Antonia las usaba en sus curaciones." The Spanish text flows beautifully. "While he slept, Diego breathed the vapors of her medicinal herbs." Here, we strongly feel her connection with his unconscious world. Even while he slept, her healing was going on. Even while he was totally unaware, she had the enormous power of bringing him back to life, of nurturing him.

I've lived in this country for a long time—New York, Los Angeles, the Midwest; many of our children here are being raised by Latin American healers. A lot of baby-sitters are nurturing our children from the way they learned in their own culture, which, even in Latin America, we don't appreciate as much as we could, or should, or must, in order to become a healthier continent.

"During the day he played in the jungle. The animals were his friends." Again, Diego is being harmonized with nature. As he's playing in the jungle, there's a snake, a symbol of healing in many cultures, overseeing him, not hurting him. This illustration is never referred to in the text, but you see it immediately. The snake is not a fierce animal threatening Diego's life; it is the symbol of healing, of Antonia's healing.

In the rest of the book, many references are made to Mexican life and history, such as *El Dia de Los Muertos,* which is very close to ancestor worship. Mexicans have a different perception of death than— I would dare say—the rest of Latin Americans. Mexicans have made a very interesting synthesis of the indigenous culture and the Christian values that were superimposed.

The book's illustrations also show the different social strata within the Mexican culture. Diego's family is rich. When he comes back, we no longer see a little hut in the mountains but a huge house where the furniture is bigger than he is. Diego writes all over the walls, so his father decides to give him a room full of blackboards where he can paint at his leisure. Does that happen to any little Mexican boy? In a subtle way, the book is showing you the economic extremes of the culture. Diego loved Mexico, he loved everything about it, and he painted everything, including soldiers killing workers on strike in the city streets. His travels to Europe leave him bored and nostalgic to come back to Mexico. Eventually the book ends, "Diego Rivera became a famous artist. His paintings made people proud to be Mexican. They still do."

CONCLUSION

I leave you with that as a last little hint on how to evaluate books about the Latino experience. Could this book make children feel proud to be part of the culture? I know this comes dangerously close to didacticism. I don't mean that we need only positive role models from a culture. More than anything, we need authenticity. This culture is full of extremes—we don't need sentimentality, we don't need romanticism, but we do need a view from somebody who has gone beyond the surface of the culture and can give children a sense that even in the midst of difficult life conditions, this is a good culture to be part of.

Latino children in schools all over our country are growing up in a dual reality, home and society, of which school is a part. These two realities are very different from each other, oftentimes presenting contradictory values which, if unresolved, remain in conflict throughout an individual's life. We as librarians and as teachers can assist children in starting to bridge the gap between contradictory values that growing up bicultural/bilingual often—I would say always—involves. In my experience, if such contradictions are dealt with and worked with, and if children are assisted and supported with understanding and caring by knowledgeable adults on both sides, a bicultural heritage enriches and enlarges life.

Authenticity in Latino children's literature is an important concept, which more often than not can only be initially identified as a feeling. Developing one's sensitivity to cultivate such a feeling can be difficult, but it's not impossible with the help of adult Latino and Chicano literature (and here I have to say that I include the word Chicano because now we *have* a body of Chicano literature, that is, literature produced in English, in this country, by people who are culturally Latinos). Children's literature specialists may be familiar with names such as Gary Soto, but they should also read adult literature such as Gloria Anzaldua's *The Borderlands/La Frontera*, a fantastic book that cuts across gender and ethnicity into just the pure passion of words. She also has edited *Making Face, Making Soul*, a book of essays by women of varied ethnicities. We have Sandra Cisneros with *My Wicked, Wicked Ways* and *The House on Mango Street*. We have Rudolfo Anaya writing *The Heart of Aztlan* and *Bless Me, Ultima*, another story of a little boy and a healer. There is a body of Chicano literature which transcends the linguistic question because we now have a population in this country of English-dominant Latinos, people who have been born here and educated in American schools before bilingual education took hold. Many of them were never taught how to read or write in Spanish, which was the language of the home, so they speak English, just like you and me. And they are producing very interesting books, at all levels, that I think would be one way for non-Latinos to access the Latino culture.

Developing one's sensitivity can be difficult, but it's not always impossible. Assisted by adult Latino and Chicano literature, along with folklore that reflects widely varied oral traditions, non-Latinos may begin the process of connection with the culture in more real terms, or should I say in more magically real terms.

REFERENCES

Banks, J. A. (1991). *Teaching strategies for ethnic studies* (5th ed.). Boston, MA: Allyn and Bacon.

Dorros, A. (1991). *Abuela*. Illustrated by E. Kleven. New York: Dutton Children's Books.

Garcia, R. (1987). *My Aunt Otilia's spirits/Los espiritus de mi Tia Otilia*. (Translated into Spanish by J. Guerrero Rea). Illustrated by R. Cherin & R. I. Reyes. San Francisco, CA: Children's Book Press.

Lukens, R. J. (1990). *A critical handbook of children's literature* (4th ed.). Glenview, IL: Scott, Foresman.

Rohmer, H. (1989). *Uncle Nacho's hat/El sombrero de Tio Nacho*. (Spanish version by R. Zubizarreta). Illustrated by V. Reisberg. San Francisco, CA: Children's Book Press.

Winter, J. (1992). *Diego*. (Translated from the English by A. Prince). Illustrated by Jeanette Winter. New York: Knopf.

HAZEL ROCHMAN

Assistant Editor
Booklist
Chicago, Illinois

And Yet . . . Beyond
Political Correctness*

THE MULTICULTURAL DEBATE

Multiculturalism is a trendy word, trumpeted by the politically correct
with a stridency and oversimplification that has provoked a backlash.
There are p.c. watchdogs eager to strip from the library shelves anything
that presents a group as less than perfect. Ethnic characters must always
be strong, dignified, courageous, loving, sensitive, wise. Then there are
those who watch for authenticity: How dare a white write about blacks?
What's a Gentile doing writing about a Jewish old lady and her African-
American neighbors? The chilling effect of this is a kind of censorship.

It's easy to laugh at the lunatic fringe. According to p.c. labeling,
I should change my name to Hazel Rochperson. I am vertically chal-
lenged (short), my husband is differently hirsute (bald), my mother is
chronologically gifted (old), my brother differently abled (brain-
injured), and some of my best friends are people of size (fat). Not at
all comforting are the same kind of euphemisms from the corporate
world: words like downsizing (firing workers). Then there's caloric
insufficiency (hunger) and ethically different (corrupt).[1]

But the greatest danger from the politically correct bullies is that
they create a backlash, and that backlash is often self-righteous support
for the way things are. Whether we are weary or indignant, we wish
the whiners would just go away. Or we focus on the absurd, and then
we can ignore real issues of prejudice and hatred that keep people apart.

*This paper is based on the introduction to *Against Borders: Promoting Books for a
Multicultural World* by Hazel Rochman (Chicago, IL: ALA Books/*Booklist* Publications).

Ethnic cleansing is the latest euphemism: It's an attack on multi-culturalism, and it isn't funny at all.

Books can make a difference in dispelling prejudice and building community: not with role models and recipes, not with noble messages about the human family, but with enthralling stories that make us imagine the lives of others. A good story lets you know people as individuals in all their particularity and conflict; and once you see someone as a person—flawed, complex, striving—you've reached beyond stereotype.

In reviewing children's books, we have to resist the extremes: the mindless conformity to the p.c. of multiculturalism, and also the backlash. As with that other current fad, "whole language," the pre-tentious jargon is only now catching up with what we've been doing all along—selecting and promoting great books from everywhere, stories that grab us and extend our view of ourselves.

Recently it has become much easier to find good books about diverse cultures. A lot more books are being published with ethnic characters and cultures that have long been ignored. There are many more books set outside the United States. Instead of just a couple of titles per season, there's a flood of them now. Some are ephemeral, just cashing in on the trend; but some tell a good story, rooted in a particular culture and reaching out to universals. The best of these change the way we see ourselves, and they shake up the world of children's books.

African-American literature, particularly, is flourishing: fiction, picture books, and history; stories of slavery and of the civil rights movement that focus not just on leaders but also on ordinary people. Styles vary from soaring rhythms to the sparest poetry. There's an increasing complexity in contemporary realistic stories, which reach beyond simple role models to confront issues of color, class, prejudice, and identity, without offering Band-Aids of self-esteem. Deborah Taylor, young adult services specialist at Enoch Pratt Free Library in Baltimore (and consultant for the African-American bibliography in my book *Against Borders*), says, "It's great that books no longer have to show us as perfect" (D. Taylor, personal communication). Coming-of-age stories can combine individual conflict with a stark social realism and also reach out to universal myth. In biography, from Sojourner Truth to Malcolm X, the struggle is not only with the racism in society but also with personal hatred and despair. There's also laughter, stretching back to the old subversive trickster tales. Comedian Dick Gregory (1989) says that once they did get around to giving us a Black History Month, "it would be the month of February, with all them days missing" (p. 424). Of course, these books about African-Americans will help promote

Black History Month and special curriculum projects. But these are great books for all of us, about all of us, all year long. You don't need a special month to make you want to read the best writers.

One of the positive effects of the whole multicultural emphasis is that—even with books that have nothing to do with ethnicity, books about making friends or sibling rivalry or mathematics—you no longer have all-white classrooms and all-white neighborhoods. The multicultural cast is becoming the norm in illustration of a concept picture book, and I seldom comment on it now in a review. The same is true of books like Alvin Schwartz' (1992) collection of children's folk verse *And the Green Grass Grew All Around,* illustrated by Sue Truesdell with wildly energetic drawings that show kids of many backgrounds. It's interesting to look at the revised editions of some of the great Let's-Read-and-Find-Out Science series, such as Paul Showers' (1991) *How Many Teeth?* first published 30 years ago. There's almost no change in the funny, informative nonhectoring text, but the illustrations by True Kelley are new: full color and multicultural. In Helene J. Jordan's (1992) *How a Seed Grows,* illustrated by Loretta Krupinski in the same series, the revised edition has a cheery African-American girl on the cover.

But it would be insulting to say that these books are good *because* they're multicultural. Betsy Hearne, editor of *The Bulletin of the Center for Children's Books,* was appalled at a recent conference to hear people recommend a book only because it was "multicultural," as if no further evaluation was needed.

In fact, one kind of book that doesn't work is the one that deliberately takes multiculturalism, and only multiculturalism, as its subject. That's like making *life* the theme. An anthology, for example, must have variety, even opposites, but it can't be just a book about variety. Otherwise, you can just throw in anything you like from anywhere and call it a book. You have to have a unity of tone, however subtle, so that the book feels like a whole. It doesn't work to have too many genres, themes, and tones, as well as places and cultures. One anthology that does have a beautiful unity is Ruth Gordon's (1987) *Under All Silences: Shades of Love,* where the poems from across the world connect people everywhere by common experience.

EVALUATING MULTICULTURAL BOOKS

How do you evaluate books across cultures? Are there special criteria? What are the pitfalls? And in a time of declining book budgets in libraries and school media centers, when librarians do have to select very carefully, how do you balance all the demands of literary quality and popular appeal and intellectual freedom and curriculum support and multiculturalism? And how do you make kids want to read?

Of course, these issues aren't new, and there are no simple answers. In the current arguments about political correctness, at times I find myself agreeing and disagreeing with everybody. If there's one thing I've learned in this whole multicultural debate, it's not to trust absolutes. I say something and then immediately qualify it with, "And yet. . . ." And it's usually because I find a book that upsets all my neat categories. That's what good books do: They unsettle us, make us ask questions about what we thought was certain. They don't just reaffirm everything we already know.

Underlying much of the debate is the demand that each book must do it all. If you think that the book you're reviewing is the only one kids are ever going to read on a subject—about the pioneers or about Columbus or about the Holocaust or about apartheid—then there's intense pressure to choose the "right" book with the "right" message. If we don't watch out, reading becomes Medicine, Therapy. We start to recommend books because they give us the *right* role models, depending on what's considered "right" in the current political climate.

The poet Katha Pollitt (1991, 1992) wrote in an article in *The Nation* that it's because young people read so little that there's such furious debate about the canon. If they read all kinds of books all the time, particular books wouldn't matter so much. The paradox is that if we give young people didactic tracts, or stories so bland that they offend nobody, we're going to make them read even less. If you're going to grab kids and touch them deeply, if you want them to read, books must have tension and personality, laughter, and passionate conflict.

The novelist E. L. Doctorow (1989, p. 90) says that one of the things he most admires about George Bernard Shaw is that he gives some of the best speeches to the characters he disagrees with. A good story is rich with ambiguity. You sympathize with people of all kinds. Read Anne Fine's funny YA novels, such as *My War with Goggle-eyes* (Fine, 1989), and you get swept up into furious family quarrels about relationships and about ideas, and neither side wins. The best books celebrate ambiguity, they glory in conflict, they make us aware that something can be itself and its opposite at the same time. This is especially so with political themes where everything can degenerate into propaganda if the characters become mouthpieces for worthy ideas. Susan Sontag (1992) sees the vitality in disagreement: "literature is a party," she says, "even as disseminators of indignation, writers are givers of pleasure" (p. xviii).

WRITERS AND MULTICULTURAL BOOKS

A library *collection* does have to satisfy all kinds of requirements. But *each book* can't do it all. Walter Dean Myers (1990) spoke at the

Columbia Children's Literature Institute in 1990, and someone in the audience asked him why he wrote a book about black kids playing basketball; it's such a stereotype, why was he feeding it? "Every book I write," he replied, "can't take on the whole African-American experience." He said he had written other books in which kids did other things. But, he said, he likes basketball; lots of African-American kids like basketball; and this one book is about that world.

One book can't carry the whole ethnic group experience. In Sook Nyul Choi's (1991) *Year of Impossible Goodbyes*—chosen as a Best Book for Young Adults last year—the Japanese occupiers of North Korea during World War II, as seen through the eyes of a young Korean girl, are cruel and oppressive enemies. Japan-bashing is a problem in the United States now, but that doesn't affect the truth of this story. You could recommend that book with Yoko Kawashima Watkins' (1986) *So Far from the Bamboo Grove* about a Japanese girl on the run from cruel Koreans after World War II, or with Yoshiko Uchida's (1981, 1991) fiction and autobiography about how Japanese-Americans were treated here during World War II.

What's more, one writer is not the representative of a whole ethnic group. Maxine Hong Kingston, who wrote the classic memoir *The Woman Warrior* (Kingston, 1976), complains about "the expectation among readers and critics that I should represent the race. Each artist has a unique voice. Many readers don't understand that. What I look forward to is the time when many of us are published and then we will be able to see the range of viewpoints, of visions, of what it is to be Chinese-American" (Sumrall, 1992, p. 77). Nor does one reviewer speak for a whole ethnic group. Phoebe Yeh, a children's book editor at Scholastic (and consultant for the Asian-American bibliography in *Against Borders*), says that she is a reader before she is a Chinese (P. Yeh, personal communication). I'm a Jew, but I can't speak for all Jews. Nor for all South Africans; not even for all South Africans who are anti-apartheid.

Every time an artist or writer does something, it doesn't have to be about her race. Sheila Hamanaka's (1990) book *The Journey* is based on her five-panel mural painting that shows the World War II experience of Japanese-Americans, including her own family, who were herded up and sent to concentration camps. It's a story of prejudice and fierce injustice, personal and official, and Hamanaka is passionate about what happened to her people. But Hamanaka also illustrates books that aren't focused on the Japanese-American experience at all. *A Visit to Amy-Claire* (Mills, 1992) is a picture book about a family, about sibling rivalry, and the family happens to be Asian-American. Recently, she illustrated a cozy picture book, *Sofie's Role* by Amy Heath (1992), about a family bakery, and there were no Asian characters at all. The illustrator Ed

Young was born in Shanghai, and he draws on the richness of his Chinese roots to give us *Lon Po Po,* the version of *Red-Riding Hood* that won the 1990 Caldecott Medal (Young, 1989). But he has also illustrated dozens of stunning books from cultures he has found here, including the illustrations that capture the mystery of Coleridge's (1992) *Rime of the Ancient Mariner,* or his witty, exuberant pencil drawings for *Bo Rabbit Smart for True: Folktales from the Gullah* (Jaquith, 1981).

Now, there are people who say that Young can't illustrate African-American folklore because he can't really know the culture. One of the big debates at the moment relates to authenticity. Of course accuracy matters. You can get a lot of things wrong as a writer, an artist, or a reviewer when you don't know a place or a culture. Junko Yokota Lewis (1992a, 1992b), who's from Japan, has pointed out some important errors in Japanese costume and custom in picture books published in the United States. For example, she shows that one illustration has characters wearing their kimonos in a style that only dead people are dressed in; another shows characters with chopsticks in their hair; a third depicts food in a manner appropriate only when served to deceased ancestors. I'm from South Africa, so I do know that culture better than the average American does, and in reviewing a book about apartheid, I might find things that you could miss. One obvious example is the use of the word "native," which is a derogatory term in Africa with overtones of primitive and uncivilized, quite different from the way it's used here. It makes me realize that I must miss things when I review books about, for example, Japan, or about Appalachia.

And yet . . . that isn't the whole story. Sometimes I worry that I know too much, that I can't see the wood for the trees, that steeped as I am in the South African culture, I can't always know what an American child doesn't know. Would an American reader be confused by something that I take for granted? One of the things that does help me is that I no longer live in South Africa, so to some extent I can see things from outside as well as in—from both sides of the border.

But what about those who say that an American can never write about Japan, that men can't write about women, that Chinese Ed Young cannot illustrate African-American folklore? In fact, some take it further. Only Indians can really judge books about Indians, Jews about Jews. And further still, you get the extreme, whites should read about whites, Latinos about Latinos, locking us into smaller and tighter boxes.

What I hear echoing in that sort of talk is the mad drumbeat of apartheidspeak. Apartheid, which means "separate development," made laws on the basis of so-called immutable differences. Not only should whites and blacks be kept absolutely apart and educated separately, but among blacks, each "tribe" should be separate, so that Zulus should live only with Zulus and be taught in Zulu about Zulus and to do things that only Zulus do. The apartheid planners wrote that all most blacks could do was simple manual labor, that science and abstract thinking weren't part of their culture, and that their training should prepare them to be good servants. It's so absurd that it's hard to believe so much of it was carried out, and with untold suffering to millions. The white government set up separate "homelands" for each tribe, forcibly uprooted millions of people from their homes, and resettled them all "together with their own kind" in a barren Gulag in the veld.

As a white privileged child growing up in that society, I didn't read books about black people. I didn't dream that there could be such books. Even the newspapers didn't have stories or photographs that showed a black person as an individual with a personal life. If "natives" were mentioned, they were seldom given names, and never second names. There was no television; radio was state controlled. The effect of that separation and that censorship was that I couldn't imagine the lives of black people. And that's exactly what the racist government wanted.

When I went back to South Africa in 1990, I interviewed Nadine Gordimer for *Booklist* at her home in Johannesburg, before she won the Nobel Prize for Literature. I asked her if she felt that as a white she could write about black experience; how she answered those who said she was using black suffering. She got angry. "How does a writer write from the point of view of a child?" she said. "Or from the point of view of an old person when you are 17 years old? How does a writer change sex? . . . How could the famous soliloquy of Molly Bloom have been written by James Joyce? Has any woman ever written anything as incredibly intimate? I mean, how did Joyce know how a woman feels before she's going to get her period?" (Rochman, 1990, p. 101).

Then this year, for Black History Month, I interviewed Virginia Hamilton, and she spoke about her frustration in not being allowed to write *outside* of the black experience. "People don't allow it; critics won't allow it," she said. "If I would do a book that didn't have blacks, people would say, 'Oh, what is Virginia Hamilton doing?' I feel the limitation," she said. "I'm always running up against it and knocking it down in different ways, whichever way I can. But I know that it's there and will always be there. I mean there were people who said in the middle of my career, 'Now Virginia Hamilton has finally faced who she is.' Well, how dare they?" (Rochman, 1992, p. 1021).

In her collections of folklore and creation stories, Hamilton brings together some of the oldest stories from many cultures all over the world: the Russian witch Baba Yaga along with the African-American Wiley and the Hairy Man. "I really think there are universals in those kinds of materials," she said. "I mean I love Baba Yaga. It's not my culture, but it's a wonderful tale" (p. 1020). She says that these stories show that "people have the same mind about certain things. They have the same fears and the same need for order. . . . In the beginning people would come inside the cave where the fire was and tell about what happened" (pp. 1020-1021).

Roger Sutton (1992), executive editor of *The Bulletin of the Center for Children's Books,* in "What Mean We, White Man?" sums it up this way: "If we cannot reach beyond the bounds of race, ethnicity, sex, sexual orientation, and class, literature is useless, leaving writers few options beyond Joni Mitchell-style confessional lyrics. Literature— language—is meant to communicate. . . . It is a way to jump out of our own skins" (p. 156).

TRANSCENDING CULTURAL BARRIERS

And yet . . . only gifted writers can do it, write beyond their own cultures. Fiction and nonfiction is full of people who don't get beyond stereotype because the writer cannot imagine them as individuals. In the apartheid history of South Africa, blacks are sinister primitives, waiting to be "discovered," their land waiting to be "opened up" to civilization. When the Zulus win, it's a massacre; when the whites win, it's a brave victory against desperate odds. More recently, images of suffering have gotten mixed in with the romantic-adventure clichés, but the view is still sensationalized and stereotyped. There's little sense of South African blacks as individuals. "Black on black violence" is the new cliché; somehow the ethnic cleansing in Eastern Europe is not called "white on white" tribal war. In fact, according to the apartheid view, Africa didn't have a history until the whites came. The mouth of the Nile wasn't there until white explorers found it. Now, it's fine to write a book about European explorers in Africa, if you make clear that that's what you're doing. But a book about African history that begins with the coming of the whites is, to say the least, incomplete.

Traveling to foreign places—or reading about them—isn't necessarily broadening. Many tourists return from the experience with the same smug stereotypes about "us" and "them." Too many children's books *about* other countries—written without knowledge or passion— take the "tourist" approach, stressing the exotic or presenting a static society with simple categories. Some writers who try to tackle a country's complex political and social issues seem to think that in a book for young people it's okay to do a bit of background reading and then drop into a country for a few weeks, take some glossy pictures, and go home and write a book about it.

There's nothing wrong with writing a book about travel, about how it feels to be in a foreign place, even about your finding a foreign place exotic or feeling an outsider there. But don't pretend you're writing about the place or the people there. If the book takes a tourist approach, just touching down from the cruise ship for some local shopping, then you get the kind of nonfiction photo-essay so common in children's literature, where the pictures are arranged so that the child—usually attired in national dress—goes on a "journey," a journey that allows the book to include some colorful scenery and local customs. Such an attitude is really a failure of the imagination. The "others" are a shadowy mass. They're not complex characters, like me, facing conflicting choices. In the popular safari-adventure "Out of Africa" stories, the black people are like the wild creatures: innocent, mysterious primitives offering respite to the jaded sophisticates of the West.

The other side of the savage primitive stereotype is the reverential. It's just as distancing, just as dehumanizing. And it's the most common form of stereotyping now. Michael Dorris (1993), a member of the Modoc tribe, acted as consultant for the Native American list in *Against Borders*. He says:

> In the world of contemporary books dealing with American Indians, the road to the unhappy hunting ground is paved with good intentions. Perhaps in reaction to a previous generation's broad categorization of native peoples as savage, dangerous, or just plain odd, the modern approach to tribal societies seems a curious mixture of reverence and caution, with a heavy dollop of mysticism thrown in for ethnic flavor. (p. 219)

He says that we don't get

> a complex view or a matter-of-fact attitude toward everyday life, past or present. . . . Historical Indians seem always teetering on the verge of extrasensory perception. Their dreams prognosticate with an eerie accuracy that any weather reporter would envy. They possess the convenient ability to communicate freely with animals and birds, and they demonstrate a knack for nature-based simile. In the politically correct vocabulary of multiculturalism, native Americans of whatever tribe or period tend to be an earnest, humorless lot, stiff and instructive as museum diorama.
>
> In other words, quite boring.
>
> As a child, I seldom identified with Indians in books because for the most part they were utterly predictable in their reactions to events. They longed for the past, were solemn paragons of virtue, and were, in short, the last people I would choose to play with. (p. 219)

The African-American poet Lucille Clifton (1991, p. 8) attacks the reverential stereotyping in her poetry collection *Quilting:*

. . . the merely human
is denied me still
and i am now no longer beast
but saint.

Of course it's great to read about your own culture and recognize yourself in a book, especially if you have felt marginalized and demonized. The writer Jamaica Kincaid, who grew up in Antigua, talks about the joy of finding the books of fellow Caribbean Derek Walcott, the 1992 winner of the Nobel Prize for Literature: "I thought we were just part of the riffraff of the British Empire until I read this man and thought: 'Oh yes, that is me. That is us.'" (Rule, 1992, p. C30). When I first read Doris Lessing's (1965, 1988) *African Stories*, such as "The Old Chief Mshlanga," I suddenly recognized things about myself that I hadn't been conscious of. I didn't find role models, but I understood how apartheid had conditioned me when I was growing up. One of the things Lessing gets perfectly is the way other people's languages always sound not only foreign but "uncouth" and "ridiculous." She's also hard on the sentimentalists who think you can just put things right with "an easy gush of feeling."

Now, I also get immense pleasure and the shock of recognition when I read Sandra Cisneros' (1989) stories in *The House on Mango Street* about a young Chicana girl, Esperanza, coming of age in Chicago. Esperanza says that her great-grandmother "looked out of the window her whole life, the way so many women sit their sadness on an elbow" (pp. 10-11). That image makes me catch my breath. It makes me think of so many strong women trapped at home. I remember my mother-in-law, an immigrant from Lithuania, well-educated, spirited, but a stranger, who got stuck in the rigid role prescribed for her in Cape Town's Jewish community. She used to sit like that, chin in her hands, elbows on the table, angrily watching us eat the food she'd cooked.

Amy Tan's (1989) *The Joy Luck Club* does give you an idea of what it's like to grow up Chinese-American, and that is a good reason to read it. It's important for Asian-Americans to read about themselves in books, and it's important for everybody else to read good books about them. It does show women struggling for independence, and that does give me pleasure. But it isn't reverential; the people aren't always wise and admirable. The extraordinary success of *The Joy Luck Club* has little to do with our need to know about "other" cultures or our own. This book is a best-seller because, rooted as it is in the Chinese-American experience, it explores the complexity and conflict, the love and anger, between mothers and daughters everywhere.

I love the Yiddish idiom and the shtetl setting in the stories of Isaac Bashevis Singer; he makes me laugh and makes me remember my mother's stories and how she loves books and he gives me a sense of my family and who I am. But that's only part of it. And just as I love Sandra Cisneros, so non-Jews can find themselves in the humor and humanity of Singer's stories.

I was on the U.S. IBBY committee that selected Virginia Hamilton as the 1991 U.S. nominee for the international Hans Christian Andersen Award. When the nomination was announced, some people said that she didn't have a chance of world recognition because foreigners wouldn't understand her, wouldn't read her, wouldn't translate her. She was too idiomatic, too difficult, too local, they said. They were wrong. She won. And, in fact, her books have been widely read in countries such as Japan for years.

CHILDREN AND MULTICULTURAL BOOKS

We're too quick to say, "kids won't read this." We each live in a small world and talk to people like ourselves and reinforce each other, and we think everyone agrees with us. If you choose good stories and if you promote them, it's not true that books in translation or about foreign cultures are only for the "gifted," that young people won't read books with a strong sense of a foreign place. Singer (1977, p. 13) says that the opposite is true, that the more a story is connected with a group, the more specific it is, the better. In an opening note to *When Shlemiel Went to Warsaw*, he says, "in our time, literature is losing its address" (Singer, 1968). That's such a wonderful pun—losing its sense of place, its identity, and because of that, losing its ability to speak, to address, an audience. Singer says that in writing for children, he's not concerned with using only words that the child will understand. "A child will not throw away a book because there are a few words that he does not understand. . . . A child will throw away a book only if . . . it . . . is boring" (Singer, 1977, pp. 14-15). E. B. White said the same about *Charlotte's Web*. "Children are game for anything," he said. "I throw them hard words, and they backhand them over the net. They love words that give them a hard time" as long as they are interested in the story (Plimpton, 1988, p. 20; Gherman, 1992, p. 93).

It's obvious that for mainstream young people, books about "other" cultures are not as easy to pick up as *Sassy* magazine, or as easy to watch as "Beverly Hills 90210." And, in fact, they shouldn't be. We don't want a homogenized culture. If you're a kid in New York, then reading about a refugee in North Korea, or a teenager in the bush in Africa, or a Mormon in Utah involves some effort, some imagination, some opening up of who you are.

Stories about foreign places risk two extremes: either they can overwhelm the reader with reverential details of idiom, background, and custom; or they can homogenize the culture and turn all the characters into mall babies. There's always that tension between the particular and the universal, between making the character and experience and culture too special, and making them too much the same. On the one hand, we don't want to be bogged down in reverential details about the way of life and the deep mystical meaning of everything the protagonist sees; we don't want to wade through thickets of idiom, background, and culture before we can get to the story. And yet . . . Elizabeth Laird's

(1992) exciting story *Kiss the Dust*, about a Kurdish teenager caught up in the Iran-Iraq War in 1984, has almost too little to do with Kurdish culture. We are quickly swept up into a fast-paced refugee story about someone—just like us—forced to flee home, school, safety. There's nothing wrong with the story, and kids will grab it for the adventure, never doubting for a moment that she'll make it through the mountains and camps to safety.

A much better book is *Shabanu, Daughter of the Wind*, by Suzanne Fisher Staples (1989), about a young Muslim girl living with her nomadic family in the desert of Pakistan. Shabanu has spirit and intelligence and that's dangerous in a girl, especially when at the age of 12 she's promised in marriage to an old man. As we come to care for Shabanu and what happens to her, we imagine what it must be like to be her. At the same time, the story is rooted in the particulars of her culture, and the sense of her place is deeply felt. The important thing is that there's no sense of the exotic; the desert is very much there but not as scenery or travelogue. This book is remarkable in showing a sense of individual personality within a tight social structure. Through Shabanu's first-person, present-tense narrative, we see the diverse, complex inner lives of her family, as well as their strictly defined cultural roles. Her father is as trapped as she is, loving her proud spirit, suffering even as he battles her into submission. As many of us do, she finds a mentor in the extended family. Her strong aunt shows Shabanu that she has a choice and tells her that no one can reach her inner self. Shabanu's culture locks her up, but inside she can be free.

Shabanu has a glossary, but I didn't know that until I got to the end of the book. I didn't need it. I got swept up into the world of Shabanu, gave myself over to the story, and even if I didn't understand every single nuance and every foreign expression, I got meanings from the context. I can't believe that reviewers object to the "Briticisms" in a book from England. That's what makes a world; and if you don't get every detail, so what? As a child in South Africa, I loved the Briticisms and I loved the Yankee talk in American movies and books; they were a draw, not a barrier.

When I was working on editing the anthology *Somehow Tenderness Survives: Stories of Southern Africa* (Rochman, 1988), both my editor Charlotte Zolotow and I were reluctant to have a glossary. We felt that readers would get the meaning of strange words from their context. If you know there's a glossary, it makes you stiff and wary instead of allowing you to give yourself over to the world of the story. What persuaded us that we did need a glossary was the fact that the racist categories and insults needed clarification. Americans didn't know that "kaffir" was the worst insult, the equivalent of "nigger" here; they didn't know that "native" is derogatory. In fact, it's a sign of the shame of apartheid that it has spawned such a list of racist names.

CONTROVERSIAL TOPICS IN CHILDREN'S BOOKS

I started this paper with a joke about names. And yet . . . what you call people does matter, especially in a society where groups are angry and divided. When Malcolm Little dropped the last name which had been given to his family by slave owners and took on X to stand for his lost African heritage, he was making a powerful statement about his identity. His renaming was like a rebirth: He was freeing himself from the self-hatred that kept him enslaved. He was rejecting the white mainstream that rejected him (X & Haley, 1965). To call a man a "boy," as they do in South Africa, is a vicious racist insult. Many whites there never learn the last names of their servants; the woman who looks after their children is "the girl." If servants are nameless, they aren't people.

Books about apartheid, about slavery, about the Holocaust, can be grim. Do you give young people books about racial oppression and mass suffering? How do you evaluate such books? Young people want to know about these things, and it is important that they should know. But whether it's fiction or nonfiction, the account should not exploit the violence; it shouldn't grab attention by dwelling on sensational detail. Nor should it offer slick comfort; the Holocaust did not have a happy ending. Nor should it fall back on exhortation and rhetoric; after a while, words like "horror," "atrocity," "terrible" cease to mean anything.

The best stories tell it from the point of view of ordinary people like Anne Frank, like us. A Holocaust account like Ida Vos' (1991) *Hide and Seek* is understated, allowing the facts to speak for themselves, true to the Jewish child's bewildered point of view. (Why must she wear a star? What does it mean, going into hiding?) No gimmicks such as time travel and easy escape; no harangue and melodrama. The winner of the 1992 Batchelder Award for the best book in translation, Uri Orlev's (1991) *The Man from the Other Side,* has none of the sentimentality that pervades so many children's books about the Holocaust. While the teenager's first-person account is unequivocal about the evil of the Nazi genocide, the misery of the crowded ghetto, and the stirring events of the brave Warsaw Ghetto uprising, it also bears witness to the way hunger and fear affected individual behavior. The Jews weren't an amorphous group of victims and heroes. Some were brave; some weren't; there were traitors among them. Many Poles were anti-Semitic; some were indifferent; but some transcended prejudice. In Lyll Becerra de Jenkins' (1988) *The Honorable Prison,* the political terror in a Latin American country is personalized through one girl's experience. When her family is placed under house arrest because of her father's politics, though she loves her father and admires his ideals, there are times when she hates him, even wishes he would die, so that the family can go free. Stories like these defeat stereotype. They overcome the evil institution, not by making the character a heroic role model or a proud representative of the race, not by haranguing us with a worthy cause, but by making the individual a person.

CONCLUSION

I have tried to take all these criteria into account for my book *Against Borders: Promoting Books for a Multicultural World* (Rochman, 1993). At first I felt overwhelmed by the demands of political correctness. How was I going to choose the "right" books for the bibliographies and book discussions? What about all the watchdogs from everywhere who would pounce: How could you put that book in? How could you leave that title out? Even with my editors—Bill Ott, editor and publisher of *Booklist*, and Bonnie Smothers, acquisitions editor at ALA Books—and lots of wise and committed consultants, there were going to be so many *problems*.

My husband is a long-time apartheid fighter. "Not *problems*," he said, "*Riches*."

And that's really the point about the whole multicultural debate. When I lived under apartheid, I thought I was privileged—and compared with the physical suffering of black people I was immeasurably well-off—but my life was impoverished. I was blind and I was frightened. I was shut in. And I was denied access to the stories and music of the world. Groups like Ladysmith Black Mambazo were making music right there, and I couldn't hear them. I didn't know that in the streets of Soweto there were people like Nelson Mandela with a vision of a nonracial democracy that would change my life. I was ignorant and I didn't know I was ignorant. I thought I was better than someone like Mark Mathabane's mother because she spoke English with an accent; but she was fluent in four languages (Mathabane, 1986). I didn't know anything about most of the people around me. And because of that I didn't know what *I* could be.

Borders shut us in, in Johannesburg, in Los Angeles and Chicago, in Eastern Europe, in our own imaginations. The best books can help break down that apartheid. They surprise us—whether they are set close to home or abroad. They extend that phrase "like me" to include what we thought was strange and foreign. And they change our view of ourselves.

You know that old story about the man who searched for treasure all over the world and then found it right there in his own backyard?

Mythologist Wendy Doniger O'Flaherty says that the story doesn't mean that you should stay home and never go out into the world—what the story's really saying is that it's only *because* you've traveled that you can find treasure at home.[2] When you get lost in a story, when you get to care about a character, you find yourself in a new world that makes you look at yourself in a new way. You think about things you took for granted. You imagine other people's lives—and that makes you discover your own.

NOTES

[1] My main source for these terms is *The Official Politically Correct Dictionary and Handbook* (Beard & Cerf, 1992), which scrupulously documents its references to the usage of these terms.

[2] My friend Darlene McCampbell, an English teacher at the University of Chicago Laboratory Schools, told me this wonderful story that Wendy Doniger O'Flaherty (1988) told when she visited the school during Arts Week. In her book *Other People's Myths: The Cave of Echoes,* she quotes the great Indologist Heinrich Zimmer's comment on the myth of the Rabbi of Cracow: "Now the real treasure . . . is never far away; it lies buried in the innermost recess of our own home; that is to say, our own being . . . but there is the odd and persistent fact . . . that the one who reveals to us the meaning of our cryptic inner message must be a stranger, of another creed and a foreign race" (p. 138).

REFERENCES

Beard, H., & Cerf, C. (1992). *The official politically correct dictionary and handbook.* New York: Villard Books.

Choi, S. N. (1991). *Year of impossible goodbyes.* Boston, MA: Houghton Mifflin.

Cisneros, S. (1989). My name. *The house on Mango Street* (rev. ed.). New York: Vintage.

Clifton, L. (1991). Note to my self. In *Quilting: Poems 1987-1990.* Brockport, NY: BOA Editions.

Coleridge, S. T. (1992). *Rime of the ancient mariner.* Illustrated by E. Young. New York: Atheneum.

Doctorow, E. L. (1989). In B. Moyers (Ed.), *A world of ideas: Conversations with thoughtful men and women about American life today and the ideas shaping our future.* New York: Doubleday.

Dorris, M. (1993). Introduction to "Native Americans." In H. Rochman, *Against borders: Promoting books for a multicultural world* (p. 219). Chicago, IL: ALA Books/*Booklist* Publications.

Fine, A. (1989). *My war with Goggle-eyes.* Boston, MA: Joy Street Books.

Gherman, B. (1992). *E. B. White: Some writer!* New York: Atheneum.

Gordon, R. (Comp.). (1987). *Under all silences: Shades of love: An anthology of poems selected by Ruth Gordon.* New York: Harper & Row.

Gregory, D. (1989). February. In L. Goss & M. E. Barnes (Eds.), *Talk that talk: An anthology of African-American storytelling* (pp. 424-428). New York: Simon & Schuster.

Hamanaka, S. (1990). *The journey: Japanese Americans, racism and renewal.* New York: Orchard Books.

Heath, A. (1992). *Sofie's role.* Illustrated by S. Hamanaka. New York: Four Winds Press.

Jaquith, P. (1981). *Bo Rabbit smart for true: Folktales from the Gullah.* Illustrated by E. Young. New York: Philomel Books.

Jenkins, L. B. de. (1988). *The honorable prison*. New York: Lodestar Books.

Jordan, H. J. (1992). *How a seed grows*. Illustrated by L. Krupinski. New York: HarperCollins.

Kingston, M. H. (1976). *The woman warrior: Memoirs of a girlhood among ghosts*. New York: Knopf.

Laird, E. (1992). *Kiss the dust*. New York: Dutton Children's Books.

Lessing, D. (1965). The old Chief Mshlanga. In *African stories*. New York: Simon & Schuster.

Lessing, D. (1988). The old Chief Mshlanga. In H. Rochman (Ed.), *Somehow tenderness survives: Stories of southern Africa* (pp. 19-35). New York: Harper & Row.

Lewis, J. Y. (1992a, September). *Looking beyond literary and visual images to raise the level of cultural consciousness*. Paper presented at the Chicago Children's Reading Round Table Conference.

Lewis, J. Y. (1992b). Reading the world: Japan. *Book Links, 1*(4), 24-26.

Mathabane, M. (1986). *Kaffir boy: The true story of a Black youth's coming of age in Apartheid South Africa*. New York: Macmillan.

Mills, C. (1992). *A visit to Amy-Claire*. Illustrated by S. Hamanaka. New York: Macmillan.

Myers, W. D. (1990). Talk presented at Columbia Children's Literature Institute, New York.

O'Flaherty, W. D. (1988). *Other peoples' myths: The cave of echoes*. New York: Macmillan.

Orlev, U. (1991). *The man from the other side* (H. Halkin, Trans.). Boston, MA: Houghton Mifflin.

Plimpton, G. (Ed.). (1988). E. B. White. In *Writers at work. The Paris Review interviews* (8th series) (pp. 1-23). New York: Viking.

Pollitt, K. (1991). Why do we read? *The Nation*, September 23.

Pollitt, K. (1992). Why do we read? In P. Berman (Ed.), *Debating P.C.: The controversy over political correctness on college campuses* (pp. 201-211). New York: Dell.

Rochman, H. (Ed.). (1988). *Somehow tenderness survives: Stories of southern Africa*. New York: Harper & Row.

Rochman, H. (1990). The Booklist interview: Nadine Gordimer. *Booklist, 87*(2), 100-101.

Rochman, H. (1992). The Booklist interview: Virginia Hamilton. *Booklist, 88*(11), 1020-1021.

Rochman, H. (1993). *Against borders: Promoting books for a multicultural world*. Chicago, IL: ALA Books/*Booklist* Publications.

Rule, S. (1992, October 9). Walcott, poet of Caribbean, is awarded the Nobel Prize. *The New York Times*, pp. A1, C30.

Schwartz, A. (1992). *And the green grass grew all around: Folk poetry from everyone*. Illustrated by S. Truesdell. New York: HarperCollins.

Showers, P. (1991). *How many teeth?* (rev. ed.). Illustrated by T. Kelley. New York: HarperCollins.

Singer, I. B. (1968). *When Shlemiel went to Warsaw & other stories*. New York: Farrar, Straus, and Giroux.

Singer, I. B. (1977). Isaac Bashevis Singer on writing for children. *Children's Literature* (Vol. 6, pp. 9-16). Philadelphia, PA: Temple University Press.

Sontag, S. (Ed.). (1992). Introduction. *Best American essays, 1992* (pp. xiii-xix). New York: Ticknor & Fields.

Staples, S. F. (1989). *Shabanu, Daughter of the wind*. New York: Knopf.

Sumrall, A. C. (Ed.). (1992). *Write to the heart: Quotes by women writers*. Freedom, CA: Crossing Press.

Sutton, R. (1992). What mean we, white man? *VOYA, 15*(3), 155-158.

Tan, A. (1989). *The joy luck club*. New York: Putnam.

Uchida, Y. (1981). *A jar of dreams*. New York: Atheneum.

Uchida, Y. (1991). *The invisible thread*. Englewood Cliffs, NJ: J. Messner.

Vos, I. (1991). *Hide and seek* (T. Edelstein & I. Smidt, Trans.). Boston, MA: Houghton Mifflin.

Watkins, Y. K. (1986). *So far from the bamboo grove*. New York: Lothrop, Lee & Shepard.

X., M., & Haley, A. (1965). *The autobiography of Malcolm X*. New York: Grove Press.

Young, E. (1989). *Lon Po Po: A Red-Riding Hood story from China*. New York: Philomel Books.

In Conclusion

It is amazing, in a three-day conference devoted to the subject of evaluating books for children and young adults, that not one speaker has given much attention to the question, "What is a good book?" It reminds me of the first day of a college English class where the professor, the late, lamented Beverle Houston, sat at the head of the seminar table, blew an impressive smoke ring into the air above us, and majestically announced that there was no such *thing* as a good book. We senior English majors, each passionately attached to various books, authors, or centuries, were aghast, dismayed at the thought that four years of fancy education had just gone down the drain.

What Beverle meant, of course, was that we can't call a book "good" in the same sense we can call it "red-covered," or 247 pages long, or fiction, or "by Jane Austen." These are all objective qualities (although the post-structuralist French would even question that), while an assessment of a book's value is a subjective response. Checklists of evaluative criteria may help us in defining our questions about a book, but our answers will always tell us more about ourselves than about the book in question. When Gertrude Stein was asked by *The Little Review* for her assessment of modern art, she replied, "I like to look at it," a response that is facile but entirely to the point.

The review editors who led off the conference discussed how to get books to the librarians who will want them; librarians Janice Harrington and Janie Schomberg talked about what they wanted from reviews. Violet Harris, in her critique of the whole-language classroom, articulated yet another audience for reviews. Each of these speakers addressed the pragmatic matrix of children's book reviewing: how can the reviewing process most effectively get books to children? Betty Carter and Dorothy Briley looked more closely at what reviews do and do not do: Carter suggests an implicit bias in the review media against informational nonfiction; Briley measures the commercial impact of reviews, and also wishes the reviewers could come to some agreement as to what constitutes adequate documentation in informational books for children. Catherine Mercier and Barbara Kiefer brought the language of formal criticism into our debate, reminding us that the "practical criticism" of reviewing has a base in critical theory, however far removed words such as "charming" can be from considerations of "synchronic paradigmatic shifts." Graciela Italiano and Hazel Rochman brought reviewing into the arena of social criticism, translating headlines about multiculturalism and political correctness into questions with practical consequences for library materials selection.

Despite divergent approaches, the papers together demonstrate a healthy synthesis of thinking about children's literature that has long characterized the best library school teaching and research in the subject. Unlike English and even education departments that have recently "discovered" children's literature as a newly appropriate field for aesthetic gleaning, library education has been looking at children's books for nearly a century. And by necessity, that research has encompassed manifold approaches in which the practical, political, and aesthetic inform and enrich each other to the benefit of both children and books.

Good reviewers know that specifics in evaluation yield far more than sweeping adulation or offhand dismissal. The question, "Is it a good book?" seems at once too big to be useable, and too petty to be useful. Perhaps, though, a Platonic conception of a "good book" is itself a useful drive, pushing and provoking questions that force us to specify our own ideas of what a "good book" is.

What is a good book? Just because there's no answer doesn't mean it's not a good question.

Roger Sutton
Editor

Contributors

DOROTHY BRILEY is Editor in Chief and Publisher of Clarion Books, a children's book imprint of the Houghton Mifflin Company located in New York City. An editor of children's books since 1962, she began her career at the Viking Press Jr. Books department, where she worked for both Annis Duff and Velma Varner, and later went to Lothrop, Lee & Shepard Books and to J. P. Lippincott Company. She has worked actively on behalf of the International Board on Books for Young People.

BETTY CARTER, Associate Professor in the School of Library and Information Studies at Texas Woman's University, teaches classes in young adult and children's literature. She is a board member of the Young Adult Library Services Association and is president of the Assembly on Adolescent Literature of the NCTE. In 1990, she and Richard F. Abrahamson published *From Delight to Wisdom: Nonfiction for Young Adults*.

ILENE COOPER is the Children's Books Editor at *Booklist* magazine, the review journal of the American Library Association. With ten years' experience as a children's librarian at the Winnetka Public Library District, she is the author of numerous books for children, including the series *Kids from Kennedy Middle School* and *Hollywood Wars*. She has also written for television and for eight years was a consultant for ABC's Afterschool Specials.

JANICE N. HARRINGTON is Head of Youth Services at the Champaign Public Library and Information Center, Champaign, Illinois. She holds a B.S. in Education from the University of Nebraska and a M.L.S. from the University of Iowa. She has published on multiculturalism in library programming, storytelling, and children's reference services, and has taught at Indiana State University at Terre Haute and the University of Illinois at Urbana-Champaign.

VIOLET HARRIS received her Ph.D. from the University of Georgia. She is currently an Associate Professor at the University of Illinois at

Urbana-Champaign. Her research interests include children's literature, multiethnic children's literature, and literacy materials created for African-American children prior to 1950, which she discusses in a book of essays she has edited, *Teaching Multicultural Literature in Grades K-8.*

BETSY HEARNE is Editor of *The Bulletin of the Center for Children's Books* and Associate Professor at the Graduate School of Library and Information Science at the University of Illinois, Urbana-Champaign. Her publications include *Choosing Books for Children: A Commonsense Guide, Beauty and the Beast: Visions and Revisions of an Old Tale,* and several children's and young adult books, among them *Eli's Ghost* and *Love Lines: Poetry in Person.*

GRACIELA ITALIANO is a lecturer in the Department of Ethnic and Women's Studies at California Polytechnic University, Pomona, California. She has been active in bilingual programs and cross-cultural education, has spoken widely at conferences and workshops on both subjects, has reviewed for *School Library Journal,* and is the co-author (with M. Matthias) of "Louder than a Thousand Words" in Baton's *Signposts to Criticism of Children's Literature.*

TREVELYN JONES has been Book Review Editor for *School Library Journal* since 1982. After receiving her M.L.S. at Case Western Reserve University, she worked for 16 years as a children's and young adult librarian in the Garden City Public Library in New York. The chair of the Newbery Committee in 1987, she is a frequent speaker at conferences and workshops on issues of reviewing.

BARBARA KIEFER is an Associate Professor at Teachers College, Columbia University, where she teaches courses in reading and children's literature. Originally trained in art education, she is particularly interested in the role that picture books play in developing children's literacy and aesthetic understanding. She has published articles and book chapters about reading and children's literature and is co-author of *An Integrated Language Perspective in the Elementary School: Theory Into Action.*

JOANNA RUDGE LONG has been the Young Adult/Children's Book Editor of *Kirkus Reviews* since 1986. She has also worked at New York Public Library, where she was a children's librarian and a Borough Community Specialist, and at a number of public and school libraries in New Jersey. She has taught children's literature at Rutgers University and Trenton State College; worked for Holiday House, a publisher of children's books; and has been a first-grade teacher and storyteller.

CATHRYN M. MERCIER is Assistant Professor and Associate Director of the Simmons College Center for the Study of Children's Literature. She works with the Boston Parents Paper to produce a monthly "Bookviews" column and reviews regularly for *The Five Owls*. Her recent publications include an outline of the children's literature graduate program in *Teaching Children's Literature: Issues, Pedagogy, Resources* and, with Susan P. Bloom, a biocritical study, *Presenting Zibby Oneal*.

HAZEL ROCHMAN has worked as a journalist in South Africa, a teacher in England, and a school librarian at the University of Chicago Laboratory Schools. Since 1984 she has reviewed for the Books for Youth section at *Booklist*, where she is Assistant Editor. She is the editor of *Somehow Tenderness Survives: Stories of Southern Africa* and author of two books, *Tales of Love and Terror: Booktalking the Classics Old and New*, and *Against Borders: Promoting Books for a Multicultural World*, from which her essay here is drawn.

JANIE R. SCHOMBERG, a school librarian since 1970, is currently School Library Media Specialist at Leal Elementary School in Urbana, Illinois. She was chair of the American Association of School Librarians Publications Advisory Committee and recently co-chaired the writing committee of the newly published Illinois School Library Media Program Guidelines. She serves on the Library Book Selection Service Intermediate Selection Committee and has reviewed books for *School Library Journal*.

ANITA SILVEY became the Editor in Chief of *The Horn Book Magazine* in 1985 following a career in book and magazine publishing. In 1989 Ms. Silvey launched a new publication, *The Horn Book Guide to Children's and Young Adult Books*. She lectures throughout the United States and Canada, teaches at Simmons College Graduate School of Library Science, publishes widely, and is currently editing *The Reader's Companion to 20th Century Children's Literature*, to be published in 1994.

ROGER SUTTON is Executive Editor of *The Bulletin of the Center for Children's Books*. He received his M.A. from the Graduate Library School at the University of Chicago and worked as a children's, young adult, and branch librarian. He was the young adult columnist for *School Library Journal* for several years, has lectured widely and published frequent articles on controversial issues in children's literature, and has contributed regularly to the *New York Times Book Review*.

INDEX